Jean-Charles Stasi

Dunkirk 1940
OPERATION DYNAMO

THE EVACUATION OF 340,000 BRITISH AND FRENCH SOLDIERS TO ENGLAND

HEIMDAL

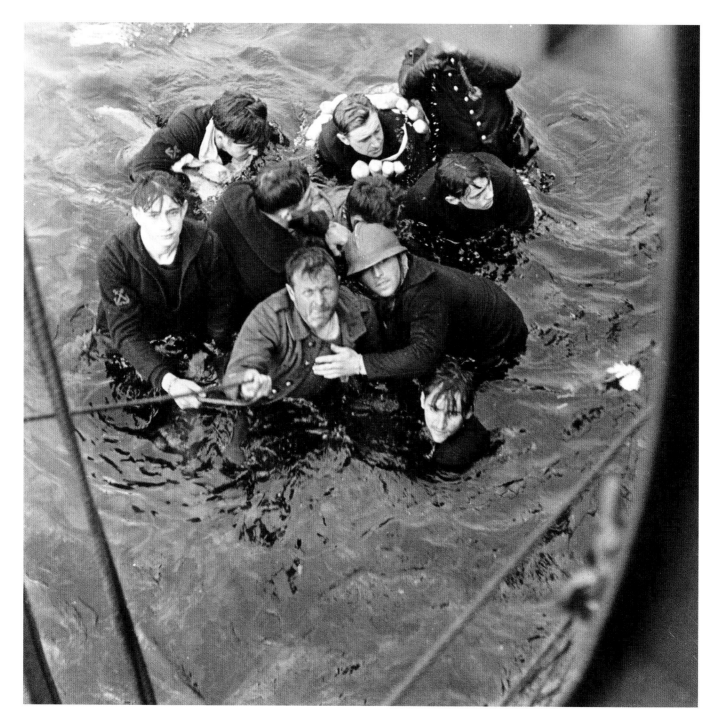

Texts: Jean-Charles Stasi
Project leader: Jean-Charles Stasi
Translation: Lawrence Brown
Format and maps: Paul Gros
Colour profiles: Thierry Vallet

Above and following page: On Thursday 30 May 1940, as it was carrying off over a thousand men, the torpedo boat *Bourrasque* hit a magnetic mine. The *Branlebas*, following closely behind, stopped its engines and put down its lifeboats in order to save the men on board the stricken destroyer. (ECPAD.)

Éditions Heimdal
BP 61350 - 14406 BAYEUX Cedex
Tél: 02.31.51.68.68   Fax: 02.31.51.68.60
E-mail: communication.heimdal@wanadoo.fr
www.editions-heimdal.fr

List of contents

Jean Bart's town
just before war came

A vital trading port, Dunkirk had seen its military role greatly strengthened since war was declared. At the beginning of May 1940, Jean Bart's town was a key element in the protection of the coastline of northern France and the border with Belgium.

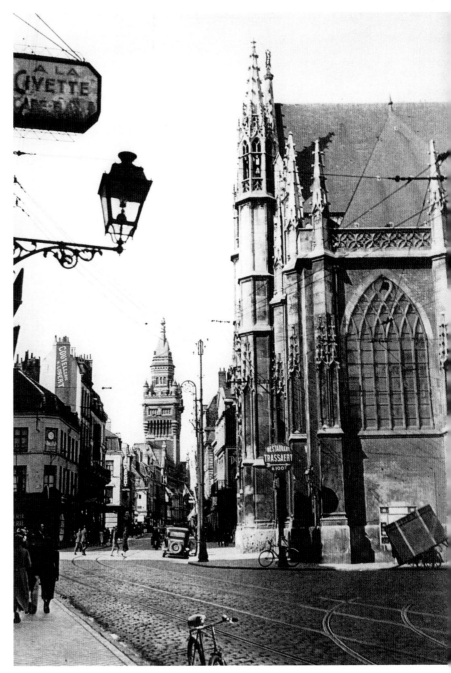

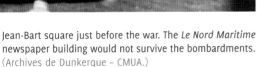
Jean-Bart square just before the war. The *Le Nord Maritime* newspaper building would not survive the bombardments. (Archives de Dunkerque – CMUA.)

Rue Clemenceau before the bombardments of spring 1940 with a view towards the town hall. (Archives de Dunkerque – CMUA.)

It is an understatement to say that Dunkirk has had an eventful history. At the beginning it was a fishing village established in the dunes around a small chapel founded in the 7th century by Saint-Eloi. Its name comes from the joining together of two Flemish words, *duin* (dune) and *kerk* (church). Since that time it has been the object of envy due to its strategic emplacement on the North Sea, a mooring site well-protected by underwater sandbanks. Thus, the town has found itself under ownership by Flanders, the Kingdom of Spain and that of England and France. In the space of a single day on 15 June 1658, and the famous "Battle of the Dunes", the town woke up under Spanish rule, French at midday and English by the end of the afternoon.

Having definitively come under ownership of the French crown in 1662, Dunkirk became a formidable fortress town thanks to work carried out by Vauban. In the 17th century, the exploits of French corsairs against British ships rendered the town famous throughout the Kingdom, notably due to the Battle of Texel in June 1694 when a small French squadron commanded by Jean Bart managed to take back dozens of ships laden with wheat that had been captured by the Dutch. This was at a time when France was suffering from hunger. It is, therefore, no surprise that the town's main square bears the name of this illustrious corsair with, in the centre, a statue made by the sculptor David d'Angers in 1845.

The 19th century saw the port grow in strength and by the 20th century it was one of France's most important ports. The war of 1914-1918 confirmed Dunkirk's military role as a place of intense naval activity. Light ships based there were tasked with covering the flank of allied troops and from preventing the German raids in the Dover Strait. However, the town was badly damaged during the war. More than two-hundred land, naval and air bombardments killed around six-hundred people and caused much damage.

In September 1939, the town of Dunkirk had a population of around one-hundred thousand. The port alone provided jobs for three quarters of the population with its naval dockyards, docks, repair yards, refineries, its crane network that numbered almost two-hundred, storage facilities, grain silo with a fifteen-thousand ton capacity and its spinning mills.

The declaration of war brought a halt to its commercial links with England that had been inaugurated in 1936. The three ships, Twickenham Ferry, Hampton Ferry and Shepperton Ferry had been requisitioned for the transportation of the British Expeditionary Force. (see chapter 2).

Throughout the following months, the people of Dunkirk became used to the black out where nightfall brought almost total darkness to the town and port, the docks merging with the quaysides and the lighthouse no longer sweeping the sea where German seaplanes laid magnetic mines.

The almost constant daily alerts due to enemy reconnaissance planes flying over the sector became part of daily life, as did the air raid shelters that sprouted up all over the place, notably in the Jean Bart square and which were called "molehills" by some locals.

Below: Jean-Bart square seen here before the war. (Archives de Dunkerque – CMUA.)

Below: An air raid shelter in Jean-Bart square, Dunkirk. From autumn 1939 onwards, these shelters sprouted up all over the town. They were nicknamed "molehills" by the locals. (Archives de Dunkerque – CMUA.)

A view of the port before the war, with the Leughenaer tower in the background (left) and the Minck (fish market, right). (Archives de Dunkerque – CMUA.)

Although Dunkirk was not strictly speaking a war port, its military role had increased since the months following the order for general mobilisation. In the spring of 1940, the town was home to the general staff of the French northern naval forces that had been created in August 1939 and whose role was as follows: the protection of British military vessels transporting men of the B.E.F. to French ports, preventing enemy naval forces from entering the Dover Strait and the east of the Channel, the protection of maritime communications in the same sector, the defence of the 1st maritime region coastline from the Belgian border to Mont-Saint-Michel.

The HQ of the French northern naval forces was in Bastion 32, situated close to the shipyards between the East Mole and the diversion canal separating Dunkirk from Malo-les-Bains. It was part of a series of bastions and curtain walls of the old Dunkirk fortifications.

Since December 1939, the commander-in-chief of the northern naval forces (abbreviated to North admiral) was 60-year old admiral Jean Abrial, who had previously commanded the Mediterranean squadron at Toulon. Admiral Abrial had direct command over the defensive sectors of Boulogne and Dunkirk, and that of Le Havre and Cherbourg. The "North" admiral's main subordinate officer was 53-year old rear-admiral Platon, commanding the Dunkirk-Calais and Boulogne sectors or the northern sector group as it was known.

Below: A map of Dunkirk and its port in 1940. It was here that the most significant events of Operation Dynamo would take place. (From a map designed by Bernard Paich for Heimdal.)

Map of Dunkirk in 1940

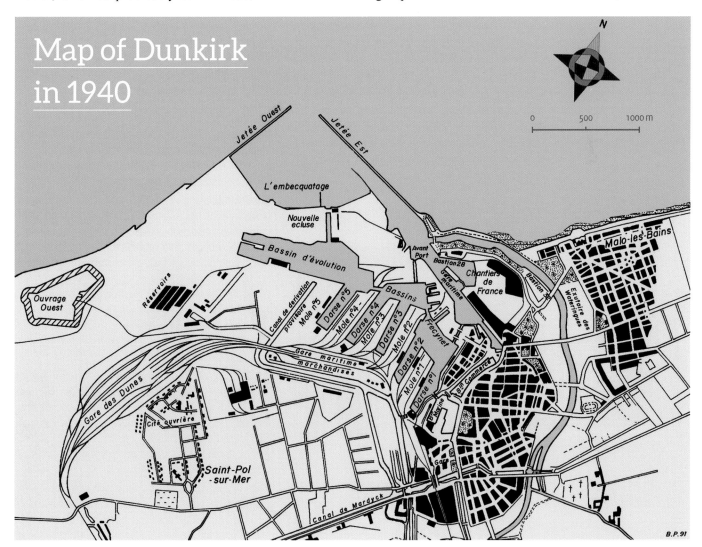

The coastal defence of the Dunkirk sector was ensured by eight gun batteries (Bray-Dunes, the Zuydcoote semaphore station, Bastions 29 to 31 of the port of Dunkirk, the West Mole of the port of Dunkirk, Bastion 28 of the port of Dunkirk, Petit-Fort-Philippe and Mardyck fort).

For the maritime defence, admiral Abrial and rear-admiral Platon could rely on several destroyer divisions (DT) based at Dunkirk but dependent on Cherbourg for supply and maintenance. Successive arrivals were the 4th DT (the *Bourrasque* and the *Ouragan*), the 11th DT (the *Courdelière*, the *Incomprise* and the *Branlebas*), the 14th DT (the *Bouclier*, the *Flore* and the *Melpomène*), the 2nd DT (the *Fougueux*,

the *Frondeur* and the *Adroit*) and finally the 6th DT (the *Cyclone*, the *Sirocco* and the *Mistral*), that arrived on 8 May. Added to these fast vessels was a group of seven modern and well-armed submarine hunters, as well as ten more or less up to date advice boats (*Amiens*, *Amiral Mouchez*, *Arras*, *Asie*, *Atlantique*, *Diligente*, *Epinal*, *Patrie*). We should not forget the minesweepers and patrol ships tasked with the surveillance of mine fields designed to block the passage of *Kriegsmarine* ships, tracking U-Boats that ventured into the Dover Strait, hunting seaplanes that laid magnetic mines and *Luftwaffe* reconnaissance aircraft.

Also under the "North" admiral's command were air and anti-aircraft forces commanded by captain Montrelay. In spring 1940, the air and anti-aircraft forces comprised of the 1st assault flotilla made up of four dive-bomber squadrons of the *Béarn* aircraft-carrier, the 5th torpedo flotilla (Boulogne), the 1st fighter flotilla equipped with the Potez 631 (based at the Marck airfield) and the II/8 fighter group equipped with the Bloch 152 (also based at Marck). Making a total of 80 aircraft.

As for the ground forces, the Dunkirk sector was occupied by the XVI army corps of general Fagalde. This consisted of two large units, the 60th infantry division, stationed south-east of Dunkirk and mostly comprising of reservists, and the 21st regular army infantry division whose HQ was at Hazebrouck.

The defence system also comprised of reservist troops from the region that were called up in September 1939 and gathered together under the Flanders defensive sector which became

This coastal defence gun bears the name of a great battle of 1914-1918, that of the Yser. This photo is from a report published by the press of the time that showed the scale of the coastal defences in the Dunkirk sector. (Archives Heimdal.)

the fortified Flanders sector in January 1940. The latter was commanded by general Eugène Barthelémy. Given the title of "commander of the Dunkirk sub-divisions", the latter was the army's representative to admiral Abrial.

It was the men of the fortified Flanders sector who, throughout the winter of 1939-1940, were put to work in setting up two defensive lines designed to halt an invasion pushing through Belgium. Finished in spring, these two defensive lines, separated from each other by 20 km and linked by access routes and comprising of

anti-tank ditches, barbed wire, minefields and some 400 fortified positions. In the event of an attack, it was also planned to flood the ground behind the dunes that was below sea level.

The *Sirocco* was one of the ships belonging to the 6th destroyer division (6th DT) that was attached to Dunkirk at the beginning of May 1940 in order to strengthen the northern maritime forces, the staff headquarters of which was based at Dunkirk. This ship was sunk on 31 May during Operation Dynamo. (Painting by Erik Groult.)

The Franco-British *Entente* just like in 1914-1918

As it did in 1914, Great Britain sent an expeditionary force to France as early as September 1939 to support its allies. The British Expeditionary Force landed in September 1939 and had a total of ten divisions by May 1940.

Above: British Expeditionary Force commander Lord Gort, seen here with Air Chief Marshal Hugh Dowding, commander of RAF Fighter Command. (IWM.)

Mechanics of the 7th Royal Tank Regiment working on Matilda Mark I tanks near Arras. The Matilda Mark I was a British light tank weighing 26 tonnes and armed with a 40 mm gun and machine-gun. Its speed did not exceed 25 kph. (IWM.)

When war was declared in August 1914, Great Britain had sent, in the name of the *Entente Cordiale*, an expeditionary force to France to assist France against the Germans.

A quarter of a century later, history repeated itself. Continuing an alliance sealed between the two countries and respecting an agreement that had been undertaken in April 1939, the first elements of the British Expeditionary Force arrived as early as September 1939. The BEF in France was commanded by General Lord Gort and was placed under the command of the French general Gamelin, commander-in-chief of the French ground forces and allied armies.

Aged 54, Lord Gort was a well-known officer who had been awarded the prestigious Victoria Cross during the war of 1914-1918. Promoted to Chief of the Imperial General Staff in November 1937, he took command of the BEF in September 1939. Lord Gort set up his general headquarters in Arras and two liaison groups were attached to French commands: the first in Vincennes at general Gamelin's GHQ; and the second at general George's HQ at La Ferté-sous-Jouarre (Seine-et-Marne).

To the first four divisions that landed in autumn 1939 were added others throughout the winter. Thus, in the first days of May 1940, the BEF had ten divisions placed in three army corps: I Corps commanded by Lieutenant-General Barker (1st, 2nd and 48th Infantry Divisions), II Corps commanded by Lieutenant-General Brooke (3rd, 4th Infantry Divisions and 50th Motor Infantry Division), III Corps led by

High ranking BEF officers. Lieutenant-General John Dill, commander I Corps, seen here with his three divisional commanders (from left to right): Alexander (1st Infantry Division), Loyd (2nd Infantry Division) and Thorne (48th Infantry Division). Promoted Vice Chief of the Imperial General Staff, John Dill was replaced at the end of April 1940 by Lieutenant-General Barker. (IWM.)

BEF men digging an anti-tank ditch in the Flines region (Nord) watched by Lieutenant-General John Dill, commander of I Corps and his staff. (IWM.)

March 1940. Men of the 1st Royal Irish Fusiliers (2nd Infantry Division) are inspected by Lieutenant-General John Dill. (IWM.)

Lieutenant-General Adam (42nd and 44th Infantry Divisions), created in April 1940. To these eight divisions were added two large reserve units, the 1st Armoured Division, which landed on 17 May and the 51st Highland Infantry Division which landed in January 1940 and was attached to the French 3rd army, positioned opposite the Maginot Line. To complete this list, we should add the three infantry divisions that were sent to France to finish their training and which had not yet received their heavy weaponry: the 12th, 23rd and 46th Infantry Divisions.

As well as these ground forces, the BEF had a Royal Air Force detachment, the Air Component, placed under the command of Air Vice Marshal Blount. The Air Component was not only tasked with supporting troops on the ground, but also with reconnaissance missions. It comprised of thirty squadrons, mainly based in the northern part of the Somme.

As laid down by the "Dyle" plan (drawn up by the French and British general staffs in

November 1939 to hold the Antwerp-Namur line in the event of a German attack), the units were deployed along the Belgian border, east of Lille, between the towns of Maulde and Halluin.

Just like their French comrades, the Tommies spent their Phoney War killing time rather than Germans. Eight long months were marked by boredom, *"the boredom of those long winter months of 1939-1940 that gnawed away at so much intelligence"*, as the French historian Marc Bloch had stated. [1] Fighting was rare if not inexistent and most of the BEF's men had not had to fire a shot before May 1940.

Luckily, there was sport, something that was greatly encouraged by the French and British general staffs. Military rugby and football matches were organised and there were even official international matches between the two countries at the French Parc des Princes stadium.

Given this dull and inactive context, it is easy to see why the British soldiers gave an enthusiastic welcome to illustrious visitors, be it the Duke of Windsor, the Prime Minister Neville Chamberlain, or the First Lord of the Admiralty, Winston Churchill; not forgetting the King himself.

Arriving on 4 December 1939 on board the destroyer *HMS Codrington*, George VI visited the BEF's infantrymen and flyers accompanied by the highest French civilian and military dignitaries. The high point of this royal visit was at Hackenberg in the Moselle, one of the Maginot Line's main fortifications. This was the moment for the King and Lord Gort to boost the tens of thousands of British troops occupying strategic positions between the Belgian border and eastern France. On 10 December 1939, the Commander-in-Chief of the BEF exhorted the men thus: *"You have been chosen to go to war as the spearhead of the British Army. Be vigilant and keep calm to the last round and to the last man and even beyond. It is not only the eyes of your country, but also those of our allies and the entire Empire that are on you."*

Determination was not lacking with the men of the BEF. Made up entirely of regular army personnel, they were well-trained and led, the main infantry divisions that made up the expeditionary force were top-tier units.

The problem lay with the armoured component. As with the French, and totally contrary to the doctrine of the German army, many light tanks were spread out in units attached to infantry divisions. These were mainly the already obsolete for its time Light Tank Vickers Mk VI, armed only with its .50 machine-gun and .303 machine-gun. The new heavy tanks, Mk II "Matilda" were not in sufficient numbers to play a decisive role in the event of a tank battle. The 1st Armoured Division was the BEF's only significant strike force as far as armour was concerned and did not have the means to fight a German Panzer division on an even basis.

Within a few days, this weakness would prove to have terrible consequences...

(1) Marc Bloch, *Strange Defeat*, first edition, 1946.

Above: A Bren Carrier in action in the Nord department. Designed in Great Britain in 1935 and made by Vickers-Armstrong, this carrier had a crew of two (driver, machine-gunner) and could carry three soldiers and their equipment. (IWM.)

Opposite: In a village in the northern France, men of the 1st Infantry Division paint their divisional emblem of a white triangle on their Bren Carriers. (IWM.)

Profile of a Light Tank, Vickers Mk VI. This light tank had a three-man crew (tank commander, loader/gunner, and driver), it was armed with a standard .303 machine-gun and a heavy .50 machine-gun. It could reach a speed of 55 km/h. (IWM.)

13-18 May. The crossing of the Meuse and the advance to the West

Three days after having attacked Belgium, Holland and Luxembourg, the Germans crossed the Meuse on 13 May 1940, penetrating into France. Fleeing the fighting, the first Belgian and Dutch refugees arrived in Dunkirk.

aspect and all the officers working their were ordered to wear their helmets.

Under a spring sun, the first elements of the French 68th infantry division left the port and headed towards Vlissingen (Holland) with the task of occupying the Walcheren islands and those of Beveland in order to cover the mouth of the Schelde.

The same day, the Dunkirk area experienced its first air raid. Bombs fell on the Mardyck airfield and the Dunes marshalling yards, but did not cause any major damage. However, the *Luftwaffe* inflicted heavy losses to the air forces and anti-aircraft defences commanded by the "North" admiral. Several men were killed at the Berck airfield. All of the AB3 squadron's planes were destroyed on the ground at Boulogne, and at the airfield of Calais-Marck, two planes had been destroyed, two men killed and many wounded.

At Borre near Hazebrouck, a twin-engine Heinkel He 111 loaded with bombs exploded in a field after having crash landed in flames, killing approximately seventy and wounding a hundred amongst the many military personnel and civilians who had gathered around the aircraft.

Three days later on Monday 13 May and after an intense aerial bombardment by over three hundred *Luftwaffe* aircraft, including many Stukas, general Guderian's tanks began crossing the Meuse. They had broken through the allied front where it was least expected, through the Ardennes that the French general staff had deemed impassable, and at the junction of the IX and II armies, commanded respectively by generals Corap and Huntziger. At the close of the day, the Germans had established a bridgehead five kilometres wide and to a depth of five to six kilometres.

Generaloberst Gert von Rundstedt, commander of *Wehrmacht* army group "A". (Archives Heimdal.)

The *5.Pz-Div* at Pont-Rémy on the river Somme, between Abbeville and Amiens. The tank in the foreground is a Panzer II light tank, armed with a 20 mm gun. (BA.)

At dawn on 10 May 1940, the German army launched its offensive in the West. At the same time in Holland, airborne troops captured bridges at Rotterdam, Dordrecht and Moerdijk, whilst in Belgium other paratroopers had landed on the Albert canal and the Eben-Emaël fort, the keystone to the Liege defences. The forces of army group A (von Rundstedt) and B (von Bock) had crossed the Belgian, Dutch and Luxembourg borders.

As stipulated by the Dyle Plan, Maurice Gamelin, the supreme commander of French armed forces, launched his three armies, and the British Expeditionary Force towards Belgium to confront the enemy advance.

In Dunkirk it was action stations. Bastion 32, the HQ of admiral Abrial, acquired a more combat

Generaloberst Fedor von Bock, commander of *Wehrmacht* army group "B". (BA.)

The Germans began crossing the Meuse on 13 May, thus breaking through the allied front.

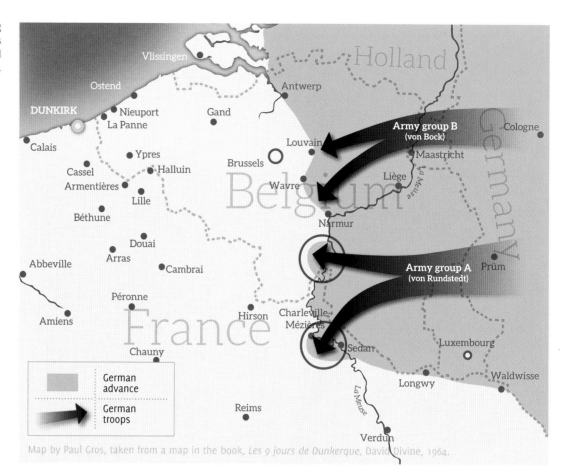

Map by Paul Gros, taken from a map in the book, *Les 9 jours de Dunkerque*, David Divine, 1964.

Below: Donchery-sur-Meuse, 13 May 1940. German troops cross the Meuse on a bridge built by engineers of the *2.Panzer-Division*. (ECPAD.)

Pushed out of their homes by the war, Belgian and Dutch refugees began heading towards Dunkirk. The wealthiest among them arrived the previous day by car, travelling along the *nationale 40* road and taking all of the available hotel rooms. The others travelled on foot or by train. Faced wih this situation, the municipality opened two emergency accommodation centres, one at the Jean-Bart secondary school, the other at the Dunes school. Added to this, an accommodation centre was set up at the town hall. Many local inhabitants opened their homes and took in families who had lost everything and who were exhausted, hungry and dehydrated by the burning sun.

Throughout the following days, this problem increased, as noted by Robert Béthegnies, who saw first hand the events unfolding in the town : *"Dunkirk was totally overrun. The streets were filled with these unfortunate people looking for a place to stay overnight. Wherever you looked there were similar sad scenes.(...) The law enforcement services, which included Belgian and Dutch police, were totally overwhelmed. Measures were taken so that cars coming from the border only parked for a short time in the area. Hotel keepers were ordered to allow refugees to stay for only twenty-four hours."*[1] Added to the

Generaloberst Georg von Küchler, commander of the German 18th army. (BA.)

May 1940. A Panzer III tank of the *4.Panzer-Division* heads towards the Channel. (ECPAD.)

thousands of refugees were Belgian and Dutch soldiers, assembled at the Jean Bart barracks where they were disarmed, albeit not without protest, by the ageing reservists of the French *511ᵉ bataillon régional*.

The reason for this continuous flow of refugees was straightforward: the lightning advance of the German troops towards the West. Applying the the *Blitzkrieg* tactics (lightning war),

using mechanised forces (tanks and aircraft) as a spearhead and not in an infantry support role, the troops of the Third Reich made huge strides. Their dive-bombers and tanks harried enemy infantry, exhausted by the marching of the previous days and lacking elements of their artillery.

It was in the sector held by the French IX and II armies that the situation was falling apart the fastest for the Allies. The Germans had opened up a breach of more than sixty-five kilometres through which poured the armoured divisions of the *Gruppe* commanded by *General der Kavalerie* Ewald von Kleist, who were tasked with taking the towns of Péronne and Cambrai, then the Channel ports.

The situation changed again quickly on 15 May. The Dutch army surrendered and the government joined Queen Wilhelmine in London. This surrender forced general Giraud's French VII army to rapidly withdraw. The surprising aspect is that despite the increasingly deteriorating military situation, there was still an atmosphere of optimism within the French high command,

German troops look at a French Hotchkiss H39 tank knocked out during the fighting of 12 and 13 May. Developed from the H35, this light tank had a crew of two and was armed with a 37 mm gun and 7.5 mm machine-gun. The Germans captured and slightly modified many of these tanks. (BA.)

as seen from these excerpts from a memo from general George's general staff, commanding the North-east front, to general Gamelin: *"Sedan breach sealed.(...) The attack appears to have been halted.(...) All prisoners state the fatigue of German troops."* General Gamelin's communiqué was similar in tone: *"The day of 15 May seems to have brought a halt. Between Namur and the the region east of Montmédy, our front, which had been knocked about, is in the process of being stabilised."*

However, the collapse of the French army was imminent. Given the scale of the German breakthrough, Paul Reynaud's government sent an urgent appeal to the British Prime Minister, Winston Churchill, during the night of 15-16 May, requesting that he increase his air support for the troops on the ground.

On the 16th, general Gamelin ordered the retreat of all French forces in Belgium. The Belgium troops were ordered to fall back on the Schelde. The men of the British Expeditionary Force were also falling back. Paul Reynaud informed Churchill by radio that the battle was lost and that the road to Paris was now open to the enemy. At the end of the afternoon, the British Prime Minister arrived in Paris by plane where he met the French president and general Gamelin.

The following day saw the continuation of the withdrawal of French and British units in action in Belgium. At the same time, the German armoured divisions, notably the *7. Panzer-Division* commanded by general Erwin Rommel, continued their push to the West, despite the exhaustion of the crews and lack of ammunition and fuel.

The flow of civilians and military personnel fleeing the fighting continued to fill Dunkirk. Over the course of five days, some twenty thousand Belgian and Dutch soldiers had passed through the town. Arriving on foot in total disorder, they told terrifying tales of the German thrust which only served to increase the state of fear and panic growing in the town.

With Gamelin informing Paul Reynaud from his HQ at Vincennes that he could no longer guarantee the safety of Paris, the British government began thinking of a possible sea evacuation of its expeditionary force. Lord Gort, in the field, ordered the bulk of his administrative and supply services of his headquarters based near Arras, to fall back to Boulogne.

Despite an audacious counter-attack led by the new 4th armoured division led by colonel de Gaulle along the Laon-Montcornet axis, general Guderian's tanks continued their advance to the West, crossing the Oise and thus opening up the way to Saint-Quentin.

On the evening of 17 May, the entire French 7th army had left Belgium. Elements of the German 6th army led by general von Reichenau had

entered Brussels which had been declared an "open city".

On Saturday 18 May, with Guderian's troops in possession of Saint-Quentin and with Rommel having reached Cambrai, marshal Pétain and general Weygand were urgently called back from Spain and Syria (Pétain was there as French ambassador (Weygand commanded French forces of the Middle-East). Upon arriving in Paris, the two men went, accompanied by Paul Reynaud, to the HQ of general Georges at La Ferté-sous-Jouarre, then to that of general Gamelin at Vincennes.

The situation was critical. Rumours of a possible evacuation of the British Expeditionary Force were growing and had reached the ears of the French high command and the President. When asked by Paul Reynaud if this were true, the British government flatly denied it.

On this same day, the military and diplomatic affairs speeded up again and took a dramatic turn of events. Dunkirk experienced its first heavy air raid of the war.

It was at 10.15pm when the air raid sirens sounded, spilling the inhabitants out of their beds and towards the nearest shelters. The anti-aircraft guns then opened up, followed by the characteristic whistling of bombs as they fell from the sky and the crash of the explosions.

Throughout the night of 18-19 May, Dunkirk was subjected to its first heavy air raid. In the early hours of the morning, the spire of the town hall is hidden by the smoke of the fires. (Archives de Dunkerque – CMUA.)

Photo taken of Dunkirk by a Coastal Command aircraft. The thick smoke is from the Saint-Pol refineries that were bombed for the first time during the night of 18-19 May. On the right we can see an American-made Lockheed "Hudson" Mk1 bomber. (IWM.)

Carrying essential items in a few bags, these inhabitants flee the République square damaged by the air raid. (Archives de Dunkerque – CMUA.)

Up until 3 o'clock in the morning, the entire town suffered fifteen successive air raids. The fires lit up entire blocks. The searchlight beams swept the sky as they looked for swastika-bearing aircraft dropping their deadly loads. *"From the very beginning of the attack, the bombers hit, amongst other targets, the Jean Bart and Guilleminot barracks that were occupied by the garrison troops, to which were added many men on leave of all arms of service who had returned the previous day. Two heavy bombs hit a building at Guilleminot, killing 42 and wounding around 200"* according to Robert Béthegnies. [2]

Bombs fell in the town centre and on the train station, creating panic amongst the refugees who continued to arrive. In Rue Félix Coquelle, a café collapsed, killing two soldiers who had taken shelter in the corridor.

Malo-les-Bains, Coudekerque-Branche and Rosendaël (eight dead) were also hit. However, it was the port that suffered the most damage. Incendiary bombs set light to the storehouses filled with bales of wool, hessian and cotton. An explosive bomb scored a direct hit on a fuel tank at the Saint-Pol refinery, sending up a huge plume of black smoke that would remain visible for several weeks. Several ships were sunk in the tidal basin. Bomb splinters mortally wounded two machine-gunners on board the *Patrie* patrol boat, moored at the departure pier.

As daylight broke, with a clear blue sky that contrasted with the horror of the night, the port was a scene of desolation. Roads and central reservations were cratered and filled with debris, railway tracks twisted by the explosions. At Moles I and II, buildings were still on fire, notably the sugar warehouse. The locks were blocked due to the destruction of the compressed air pipes required to open and close the gates, with the immediate consequence of immobilising the 6th division patrol ships and thus rendering them even more vulnerable in the event of further air raids.

In all there were sixty killed and several hundred wounded. This time there could be no doubt, Dunkirk was totally at war.

(1) Robert Béthegnies, *Le Sacrifice de Dunkerque*, published by Yves Demailly, 1947.

(2) Ibid.

Two French soldiers in the port sector look at the huge plumes of smoke rising into the sky. (ECPAD.)

4

19-25 May. The German vice closes in on Dunkirk

From 19 May onwards, it appeared that nothing could stop the advance of the German armoured divisions. The situation worsened so quickly for the Allies that Great Britain began looking into bringing its expeditionary force back home.

French sailors, in front of the curtain walls of Bastion 32, seen here during an air raid, transfer wounded sailors by ambulance to the closest aid station. Throughout the day, Bastion 32 would see more and more people arrive. The Bastion housed an up to date telephone exchange which was linked directly to Great Britain and run by British specialist personnel. (Archives de Dunkerque – CMUA.)

Without doubt, Sunday 19 May was a turning point in the Battle of France. At Dunkirk, a large number of inhabitants and refugees, horrified by the night's air raids, fled to the train station. After waiting for hours in the baking sun, they found out that the railway had been cut by the *Luftwaffe* between Albert and Amiens and that the train that had left the previous day had been forced to stop in the middle of the countryside. They could now only count on their own means to leave the battered town, where the smoke of the fires still rose into the sky. At the port, the lock gate pipes were repaired in the morning, allowing the 6th DT destroyers to up anchor and those of the 2nd DT to enter the port. Among the latter was the *Mistral* which arrived with carrying munitions and 130 mm shells.

The nine German divisions which had punched through the French front on the Meuse reorganised in the regions of Péronne and Cambrai. However, Rommel, flushed with his success since crossing the Meuse, convinced his closest superior officer, general Hoth, commander of the German armoured XV corps, to allow his *7. Panzer Division* to attack towards Arras.

Brought in three days earlier as commander of the French IX army, replacing general Corap, general Giraud was captured by the 6. Panzer Division near the village of Catelet west of Cambrai, bringing an end to the IX army, the elements of which withdrew towards the north.

Mid-afternoon, Lord Gort, increasingly preoccupied by the way events were unfolding, sent a report to London asking about the possibility of the evacuation of the British Expeditionary

The train station was soon rendered unusable by the almost daily *Luftwaffe* air raids. Like the rest of the town, it was rebuilt after the war. (Archives de Dunkerque – CMUA.)

The bomb-damaged Rue Emmery, overlooked by the spire of the town hall.
(Archives de Dunkerque – CMUA.)

Force. Churchill, still holding onto the hope of a possible Franco-British counter-attack, decided to send over the Chief of the Imperial General Staff, General Ironside, so that he could assess the situation for himself.

In Paris, *Maréchal* Pétain, called back from Spain where he was the French ambassador, was named vice-president. At the end of the day, general Gamelin was replaced at the head of the French armed forces by general Weygand. The latter, aged 73, had up to that point been commander of French forces in the Middle-East. His powers were increased compared to those of his predecessor and covered all ground, air and maritime theatres of operations.

During the night, the sirens sounded once again across Dunkirk, heralding a new air raid.

The following day, the inhabitants of Dunkirk woke up to information posters put up all over the town by the local Prefecture and which only added to the confusion and worry hanging over the town: *"All those in protected professions,*

Rue Alexandre III and the totally destroyed building of the Nouvelles Galeries shop.
(Archives de Dunkerque – CMUA.)

men of the classes of 8 to 15 liable for calling up, young people aged 16, apart from postal personnel, railways, and finance, must immediately withdraw to the Loir-et-Cher department by all possible means." This had an instantaneous effect. Thousands of inhabitants hastily packed their bags and flooded the roads, adding to the flow of refugees. Even policemen and civil servants were seen abandoning their posts in the subsequent general panic.

The same day, admiral Abrial, commander of the northern maritime forces, named rear-admiral Platon as replacement of general Tencé as governor of Dunkirk. Preparing for the coming battle for control of the port, Abrial strengthened the coastal defence batteries, ordered the flooding of the flat land around Dunkirk by opening the seawater sluices (via the Moërs canal), and decided to send off the large warships moored along the quays and which were directly endangered by the *Luftwaffe*, with a first convoy departing on the morning tide. He was proved right as the swastika-bearing bombers reappeared in the afternoon in the first of their daytime raids over the town of Dunkirk.

With Heinkels and Stukas hitting Dunkirk once again, Admiral Ramsey held an emergency conference in his HQ in the deep tunnels of Dover castle. The order of the day was as clear as it could possibly be: *"The urgent evacuation of large-scale units across the Channel".* The ports chosen were Calais, Boulogne and Dunkirk and it was estimated that ten thousand men per day could be embarked at each of these three ports. This historic meeting took place in a

From 20 May onwards, Dunkirk was bombarded day and night. Little by little, the inhabitants left the town to find shelter wherever they could. Seen here is the Quai des Hollandais with the spire of the town hall in the background following the air raid of 24 May. Only one house has been hit by an incendiary bomb and is still burning. All of the shop fronts have been closed, the shopkeepers sheltering in their cellars or already gone. Inhabitants are seen here leaving the town by bike. (Archives de Dunkerque – CMUA-Fonds Albert Chatelle.)

room that had been equipped with electric generators during the Great War, hence the name of the room, "Dynamo". This word would become the codename of the greatest maritime evacuation of all time.

General Ironside's arrival in France had the effect of making Lord Gort decide to prepare a counter-attack south of Arras for the next day.

Previously damaged during the First World War, the Saint-Eloi church was seriously damaged by the air raids of May-June 1940. (Archives de Dunkerque – CMUA.)

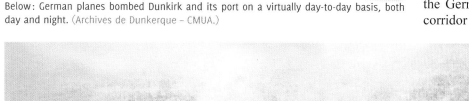

The Saint-Eloi church today. (Erik Groult-Heimdal.)

Indeed, the Commander-in-Chief of the British Expeditionary Force was increasingly sceptical as to the capability of the French forces to turn events around, attributing the current situation to errors of command.

By the day's end, after having captured Amiens, then Abbeville, the *2. Panzer* tanks led by general Guderian, reached the Channel at Noyelles-sur-Mer after a drive that saw them cover a hundred kilometres a day. The noose had been closed. From the east to the west, the Germans had opened in the allied lines a corridor some thirty kilometres wide through

Below: German planes bombed Dunkirk and its port on a virtually day-to-day basis, both day and night. (Archives de Dunkerque – CMUA.)

which they pushed infantry and artillery after the tanks. To the north of this corridor was the French 1st army, the British Expeditionary Force and the Belgian army; to the south, four French armies deployed from west to east.

Dunkirk was hit by another air raid in the evening, just as several French ships were leaving the port on the evening tide. The *Pavon* merchant ship was hit, as was the oil and supply tanker *Niger*, run aground on fire by its captain on the Mardyck sandbar. Hit by several bombs, the destroyer, the *Adroit*, was washed ashore at the beach of Malo-les-Bains. Devoured by fire, it was shaken a few hours later by a series of explosions caused by the artillery ammunition it was carrying. Its crew managed to leave the ship and went to the fort at Mardyck as personnel for the 194 mm gun battery. As for the shipwreck, it was literally cut in two by the explosions and it would now become part of the

The sugar warehouse in the port area destroyed by the air raids. (Archives de Dunkerque – CMUA.)

A view of the trading basin blocked by the wrecks of Rhine tugs, sunk by during the first air raids. The view along the *Quai des Hollandais* shows a shattered town. The background shows houses badly damaged by the bombardments. (Archives de Dunkerque – CMUA.)

battle of Dunkirk scenery until the end of Operation Dynamo. On the same night, the submarine-hunter, *Chasseur 9*, was also attacked and ended up beached at Malo-les-Bains.

Lord Gort's counter-attack began at the start of the afternoon of Tuesday 21 May. Accompanied by a small formation of French light tanks, the British tanks began hitting hard Rommel's *7. Panzer Division*, to the extent of putting doubt into the mind of the German general who spoke of a *"very hard battle"* in his diaries that were published after the war.

However, the use of the formidable 88 mm anti-aircraft guns in an anti-tank role, followed by the decisive intervention of the *Luftwaffe*, succeeded in breaking the British thrust. This failure finally convinced Lord Gort that the only thing left to do now to save the BEF was to withdraw to Dunkirk. He did not place any faith in Weygand's plan, presented to the Belgian king, Leopold III, the same day at Ypres: attacking from the north to the south to break the encirclement and re-establish a continuous front along the Somme and the Aisne. Gort's doubts were underlined by the fact that the Belgian king requested time to think before deciding to commit his army to cover the east of the future Franco-British offensive.

In the evening, as he was driving to his HQ following the Ypres conference, general Billotte, commander of the French 1st army group, was seriously injured in a car crash. Suffering from a head injury, he died two days later without ever regaining consciousness. Without general Billotte, who had been delegated authority over the British Expeditionary Force, the Weygand plan had lost its most important support.

The German threat against Dunkirk increased with each passing day. The *Luftwaffe* aircraft returned on 22 May, notably dropping their bombs on station and town centre districts. The number of dead was such that a mortuary had to be set up at the town hall and led the mayor to request the governor to evacuate the town. Rear-admiral Platon turned down the request,

having seen the consequences of the Belgian and Dutch refugee exodus as they fled the fighting.

The situation worsened on this Wednesday 22 May for the allied armies in the North. Strong German units advanced to the east and west of Arras, Boulogne was under siege and enemy tanks were no more than a dozen kilometres from Calais. The road to Dunkirk appeared to be open to the *Panzerdivisionen*, which had,

however, come up against strong resistance from some French units.

French troops continued fighting back during the morning of Thursday 23 May, notably south of Douai. However, yet again, the Stukas gave the advantage to the Germans. Right up to its very end, the Battle of France would show the incontestable and crushing superiority of the combined action of planes and tanks, sending the fighting of 1914-1918, as well as the

May 21, general Weygand leaving Bastion 32 at Dunkirk, the HQ of admiral Abrial. From 23 May onwards, admiral Abrial was tasked by Weygand with organising defences around Dunkirk. (ECPAD.)

Seen here near Bastion 32, rear-admiral Platon, who took over from general Tencé on 19 May, talks to captain Montrelay, head of the aerial and anti-aircraft defences at Dunkirk. (ECPAD.)

Above: A British Expeditionary Force motorcyclist resting near Bastion 32. (IWM.)

French air force personnel grabbing a bite to eat on the bonnet of their Peugeot near Bastion 32. (ECPAD.)

Above: British and French prisoners gathered together by the Germans south of Arras. (BA.)

theories held dear by the French high command back to the Dark Ages.

Once more, Dunkirk found itself under enemy fire, both from the air and the sea. The *Luftwaffe* and *Kriegsmarine* took it in turns to attack ships leaving the port and those attempting to enter it in order to bring in ammunition and supplies. The destroyer, *Jaguar*, was sunk by torpedoes by a German rapid *Schnellboot* in the channel west of Dunkirk, killing and wounding crew members. Survivors were picked up by the dredger *Monique Camille*. During the afternoon, the destroyer *Orage* was attacked by a large number of planes off Boulogne whilst on route to assist other French ships shelling strong German motorised columns heading to this strategic port. It was hit by several bombs, killing thirty sailors.

24 May was hit by another major event concerning the Battle of France. Whilst Lord Gort had, during the night, ordered his troops to abandon Arras and withdraw to the coast, without informing the French general staff, the advance of the *Panzer-Divisionen* towards Dunkirk was halted on the Aa canal, a mere fifteen kilometres from their objective. This was the consequence of a decision taken the previous evening by *Generaloberst* von Rundstedt, commander of army group A, and approved by Hitler against the majority of his general staff

who did not understand such a halt order (*Haltbefehl*) given that victory seemed to be there for the taking.

Much has been written on the reasons concerning this decision that, in hindsight, seems so surprising. Some state that it was due to Hitler's wish to spare the British in view of a separate peace deal, others the megalomaniac influence of the all-powerful minister of aviation Hermann Göring who wished to leave his dear *Luftwaffe* the lion's share of success in the decisive assault against the northern armies.

At the close of day on 23 May, general von Rundstedt, commander of army group A, issued a halt order along the Aa canal to his units advancing north-west. This decision would have far-reaching consequences, both for the Germans and the Allies. (Erik Groult-Heimdal.)

Above: Two British soldiers killed during the fighting south of Arras, photographed by a German war correspondent as a *Wehrmacht* vehicle passes by. (ECPAD.)

British soldiers pass through Béthune following Lord Gort's order to evacuate Arras, issued during the night of 23-24 May. (ECPAD.)

However, with hindsight, it would appear that this order was the result of more pragmatic considerations. Von Rundstedt, who had lost a large number of his vehicles in the fighting or due to breakdowns, wanted to regroup his armoured divisions following two weeks of rapid advance and ceaseless fighting. With the tanks halted, it was left up to the infantry deployed in Flanders to carry on towards the objective.

At Dunkirk, the temporary halting of the *Panzer-Divisionen* was put to good use for the organisation of ground defences. This was carried out according to the order given by general Weygand to general Blanchard who had taken over from Billotte as head of the 1st army group. The order stated that the Dunkirk area be transformed into *"the widest possible bridgehead"*, given that a Franco-British action to break the German grip seemed impossible since the retreat of the British Expeditionary Force.

As part of this order, Weygand placed general Fagalde, commander of the French 16th army corps, as commander of ground forces in the Boulogne-Calais-Dunkirk sector. He was placed under the authority of admiral Abrial and worked from Bastion 32 with the latter, where activity was increasing day and night.

On the same day, admiral Abrial issued the following order to military personnel under his command, as well as civilians: *"After having had to bypass Boulogne and Calais, which he was unable to take in the face of stubborn resistance, the enemy is concentrating his effort on Dunkirk in order to cut off the allied armies from their supply bases. Holding on to Dunkirk is essential for the success of offensives currently underway to cut off the enemy armoured units from their bases."* wrote the commander-in-chief of the maritime forces of the North, counting on *"every man to do his duty."*

Rue Clemenceau, Dunkirk, with firemen trying to put out fires caused by the air raid of 24 May. (Archives de Dunkerque – CMUA.)

However, despite the temporary halt of the German armoured divisions, the situation would continue to worsen for the Allies. Throughout the hours, the German vice tightened around Calais and Boulogne. It was in the Belgian sector that the situation was the most worrying with the German infantry reaching the Schelde and Lys rivers.

The situation continued to worsen also at Dunkirk. During the afternoon of May, a fresh

British soldiers in front of Bastion 32. This photo says much about the confusion and indecision prevalent among the Allies in the face of the rapid German advance and its increasing day-to-day threat against Dunkirk. (ECPAD.)

Exhausted from putting up a staunch resistance, the French and British defenders of Boulogne surrendered during the morning of 25 May. Seen here is a 20 mm anti-aircraft gun set up on one of the port's jetties. (BA.)

Admiral Bertram Ramsey, Commander-in-Chief of Dover Command, held the first meeting in his HQ at Dover to discuss a possible evacuation of British troops in France. (IWM.)

hail of steel and fire rained down on the town. Houses collapsed all over the place, in Rue Clemenceau, the Boulevard de la République, and the church of Notre-Dame du Sacré-Coeur was turned into a flaming torch. Malo-des-Bains, where increasing numbers of British troops were gathering in disarray , was also hit.

During the morning of the 25th, the garrison at Boulogne capitulated after putting up a ferocious fight. The defenders of the citadel showed such courage that they received the honours of war and were allowed to march with their guns in front of their victors.

With Boulogne having surrendered and Calais on the verge of falling too, there was now only Dunkirk left as an "exit" for the British Expeditionary Force.

In the afternoon, Weygand sent a telegram to general Blanchard stating that he had a free hand to withdraw his 1st army group towards Dunkirk, where Stukas attacked once again Bastion 32 and sank several dredgers.

On this same day, the British hospital ships, *Paris* and *Isle of Thanet*, sailed into the port to take on their first load of troops. This was the start of a new page in history.

In between two air raids, military personnel on anti-aircraft duty on Bastion 32, look up at the sky from the seafront fortifications. (Archives de Dunkerque – CMUA.)

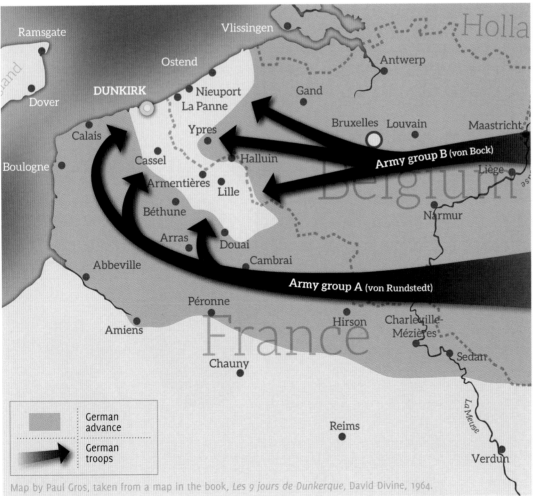

Map by Paul Gros, taken from a map in the book, *Les 9 jours de Dunkerque*, David Divine, 1964.

German advance

German troops

Above: A column of British troops makes its way up Rue des Fusiliers-Marins, leading to the port, passing a truck on flames after a *Luftwaffe* attack. The buildings seen on the left are the Ronar'c barracks housing a dressing station. (Archives de Dunkerque – CMUA.)

Opposite: The advance of the German forces by 25 May 1940. Dunkirk was now sealed off by an ever shrinking pocket.

French weapons, equipment and materiel

(Photos: Stéphane Chesneaux.)

First in service in 1887, the Berthier Mousqueton carbine had known several variants, used by the cavalry, gendarmerie, artillery personnel and colonial troops. An 8 mm calibre weapon, it was still widely issued among French troops in 1940. It was notably used by the cadets at Saumur in the defence of the bridges over the Loire on 18-20 June. It is seen here with its bayonet. (Private collection.)

MAS 38 submachine-gun adopted by the French army in 1938. It derived from the MAS 1925 and the SE-MAS 1935. A 7.65 mm calibre weapon, it had an effective range of 100 metres. It was fed by a 32-round magazine. (Private collection.)

French infantryman's uniform, spring and summer 1940. (Private collection.)

Badge of the *501e régiment de chars de combat* (tank), 501e RCC. (Private collection.)

MAC 31, 7.5 mm machine-gun magazine used on the heavy B1 bis tank. (Private collection.)

French army signals insignia (radio). (Private collection.)

French army defensive grenade. (Private collection.)

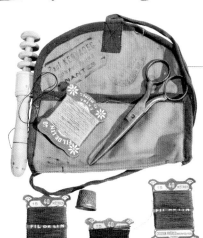

French soldier's "housewife" kit. (Private collection.)

French army offensive grenade. (Private collection.)

MAS 36 bolt-action rifle adopted by the French army in 1936 as a replacement for the famous 1886 Lebel, the rifle used by the "Poilu" of 1914-1918, as well as the Berthier Mousqueton carbine. This 7.5 mm calibre weapon had a five-round magazine and an effective range of 200 metres. (Private collection.)

Five-round charger for the MAS 36 rifle. (Private collection.)

French army motorcyclist's goggles with their storage tin. (Private collection.)

French army "Other ranks" cigarettes, 1939-1940. (Private collection.)

20 CIGARETTES DE TROUPE

French soldier's personal mess-tin, dog tag and soap. (Private collection.)

French army dressings. (Private collection.)

Medical services Adrian steel helmet. (Private collection.)

MAC 24/29 machine-gun, a staple of the French army during the Second World War. It was known by the infantry as the FM 24/29 and was well-liked by the latter. It was progressively replaced at the beginning of the 1960s by the AA-52. This 7.5 mm weapon weighed empty 9 kilograms. It had a 25-round magazine. (Private collection.)

British weapons, equipment and materiel

(Photos : Stéphane Chesneaux.)

Lee-Enfield Mk III. This short, .303 calibre rifle entered into service with the British Army at the beginning of the 20th century. It was fed by five-round chargers and had an effective range of 500 metres. It is seen here with its N°1 Mk 1 bayonet. (Private collection.)

Ammunition for the Lee-Enfield Mk III rifle. (Private collection.)

.45 calibre Webley Mark IV revolver. It was loaded via a six-chamber cylinder barrel. A well-liked and reliable weapon, it was widely issued within the British Army. (Private collection.)

Battle Dress blouse of a 50th Northumberland Division sergeant. (Private collection.)

Steel helmet of a 50th Northumberland Division soldier. (Private collection.)

British infantry Field Service Cap. (Private collection.)

British artillery officer's cap. (Private collection.)

Other rank's Tam O' Shanter, Highland Light Infantry. (Private collection.)

Issue cigarette tin containing 50 cigarettes. (Private collection.)

Regulation British Army gas mask, 1940. (Private collection.)

British Army rum jars. (Private collection.)

British artillery officer's tunic. (Private collection.)

British Army dressing, 1940. (Private collection.)

Mills N°36 fragmentation grenade. The Mills bomb first entered into service in 1915 and would remain the British Army's defensive grenade up to the beginning of the 1970s. (Private collection.)

The widely-issued Bren Light Machine-gun Mk 1. This .303 gun was fed by 30-round magazines. It is seen here with its carrying bag. The Bren entered into service with the British Army in 1937. It was an evolved version of the Czechoslovakian LMG, ZB-30 and its name is the result of the abbreviation of its place of invention (Brno manufacture and the Royal Enfield arsenal). (Private collection.)

PLAYER'S CLIPPER CIGARETTES

S.R.D.

S.R.D.

First Field Dressing

German weapons, equipment and materiel (Photos : Stéphane Chesneaux)

Mauser 98K rifle, the regulation other ranks' weapon of all of the German army's components throughout the Second World War. It is seen here with its bayonet. This 7.92 mm rifle used five-round chargers and had an effective range of 300 metres. (Private collection.)

Ammunition for the Mauser 98K rifle with pouches and transportation box. (Private collection.)

German stick grenade and transportation box. (Private collection.)

The P38 pistol was standard issue in the German army during the Second World War. This 9 mm calibre gun held an eight-round clip. Designed in the 1930s as a replacement for the aging P08 Luger, the P38 was made by Walther, Mauser and Spreewerke. (Private collection.)

The Luger Parebellum was one of the very first semi-automatic pistols. Developed by Georg Luger in 1898, it entered into production in 1900 and equipped the German army throughout both world wars. The standard model used by the German army was adopted under the name of P08, corresponding to the 1908 type, chambered for 9 mm parebellum rounds and carrying an eight-round magazine clip. (Private collection.)

German Machinenpistole 40 submachine-gun, commonly known as the MP40. Initially destined for armoured vehicle crews, its handling characteristics soon led it to become the weapon of all branches of the German army, including U-Boot crews. This 9 mm calibre weapon had a 32-round box magazine, an effective range of 100 metres and a 500-600 per minute round rate of fire. (Private collection.)

Standard issue German army gas mask with its transportation case and spare parts items. (Private collection.)

Metal case used for the transportation of Flak 18 37 mm anti-aircraft gun projectiles. The latter was capable of hitting planes at an altitude of 4,000 metres, but the Flak 18 was also used against ground targets. (Private collection.)

Rucksack belonging to a pioneer soldier of the German army. (Private collection.)

20-litre jerrycan which, as the white stencilling indicates, was made in 1940. (Private collection.)

Regulation German army mess tin and cutlery. (Private collection.)

Field dressings used by the German army in 1940. (Private collection.)

5

26 May-3 June. Nine days that put Dunkirk into the history books

At the end of the day on 26 May, the British started Operation Dynamo. This evacuation of their expeditionary force and some of the French soldiers in the Dunkirk pocket, would last for more than a week in hellish conditions.

Apocalyptic scenes greeted the British and French ships as they arrived in the port of Dunkirk. (IWM.)

Calais, 26 May. A German motorcyclist picks his way through the ruined town where the garrison had just surrendered. (BA.)

Sunday 26 May

Since dawn, the battle for the control of Calais had been raging. Following an intense artillery barrage, the German infantry went into action, supported by Stukas and tanks that opened gaps in the walls of the citadel. Despite putting up a ferocious resistance, the French soldiers could not win against an enemy superior in numbers and materiel. At the end of the afternoon, this strategic port also fell, a day after the capture of Boulogne.

Meeting at Attiches, south of Lille, Lord Gort and general Blanchard agreed to begin a withdrawal movement that night in order to establish a new line of defence behind the river Lys. The 1st army group commander also met Léopold III in Bruges, the Belgian army HQ. The King

informed him that his army was no longer capable of taking part in a counter-offensive to the east of the front, especially if it would not have the support of the British. Indeed, it appeared that the die had been cast for the latter. A telegram from the Secretary of State for War, Anthony Eden, to Lord Gort stating that the: *"only course open to you may be to fight your way back to the west where all beaches and ports east of Gravelines will be used for embarkation. Navy will provide fleet of ships and small boats... the RAF will provide its full support."*

Following the loss of Boulogne and Calais, there was only Dunkirk left as an "exit" for England. However, the increasing frequency of air raids had caused so much damage to the port infrastructure that for now, only a partial evacuation of the British Expeditionary Force was envisaged.

Shortly before 19.00 hrs, and after having been given the go-ahead by the Admiralty, Ramsey gave the order to begin Operation Dynamo in order to *"Evacuate over two days 45,000 men of the Expeditionary Force before the enemy probably puts an end to the operation."* This first contingent represented 1/5th of the some 250,000 BEF men still in France, given the fact that non-combatant elements (some 28,000 personnel) had mostly already been taken back to England via Calais, Boulogne and Dunkirk.

However, in fact Dynamo had begun several hours before the official order to start was given. Indeed, in mid-afternoon, the first troop ships had left Dover without the French high command being informed and the lead ships were already embarking troops when Ramsey's order reached them.

Ships leaving England had to run the gauntlet of fire from German artillery positions above Calais, as well as attack from the air. The

A scene of desolation after the town's capture, with abandoned vehicles, uniforms and equipment scattered across the deserted quays. (BA.)

Schnellboote also appeared from Rotterdam after a two-day absence.

Upon approaching Dunkirk, the British sailors were met with apocalyptic scenes. To the west, the fuel tanks at the Saint-Pol refineries were on fire and the flames lit up the bomb damaged quays, as well as the twisted cranes and shells of the warehouses. Whenever the thick smoke abated a little, the eye was caught by the fires all over the town.

Around 1,500 BEF men were evacuated and arrived in Dover at approximately 10.30pm; operations would continue throughout the night.

Monday 27 May

The order had been given the previous day but it was only at dawn that von Rundstedt's armoured divisions began moving again after a halt of three days near Dunkirk, the port of which they could see from the hill at Watten. There was a general feeling of optimism. *"I am very well. We are encircling the British and French in Lille. I am taking part in the south-east flank."* wrote the *7. Panzer* commander, Rommel, to his wife.

With the Germans resuming their offensive, a new meeting of allied heads was held at Cassel, thirty kilometres south of Dunkirk. Lord Gort had delegated a representative, Lt. Gen. Adam, but the Belgians were absent, however. Weygand's chief of staff, general Koeltz, informed the British that the French supreme commander expected the British Army to *"energetically take part in the necessary joint*

The military road seen from the top of Bastion 32 on 27 May. Many vehicles are seen parked around the bastion, showing the hive of activity at the HQ for the defence of the Dunkirk perimeter. (CPA.)

counter-attacks" as part of an attack to recapture Calais.

However, the French optimism failed to convince the British whose priority was more than ever the re-embarkation of their troops. This was confirmed a few hours later to Lord Gort by the Secretary of State for War, Anthony Eden, stating that his *"sole task now is to evacuate to England as much of your forces as possible."*

27 May was a day of intense activity on all levels. Around Dunkirk, the Germans increased the pressure on the French lines. Fighting continued throughout the day, notably in the areas of Bourbourg, Cassel and Bergues, finally forcing the defenders back to the second line of defence from Drincham to Herzeele.

On the eastern part of the front line, the situation of the Belgian army was increasingly critical. The German 6th army had opened up a gap in the enemy lines, thus opening the road to Bruges. After having informed his allies of his desire to lay down his arms, Léopold III signed that night a surrender protocol that would lead to a cessation of hostilities starting at 5am on 28 May.

This decision was very badly received by the allied politicians and military leaders. Apart from the fact that it left the French 1st army's flank in the air, it also led the British to speed up the evacuation as they now feared a heavy attack on Dunkirk and a general collapse of the front.

Back in Dunkirk the town was, since the beginning of the morning, experiencing its heaviest air raid so far. For over twelve hours, the bombers of four *Luftwaffe* corps arrived in waves of thirty to forty planes, dropping their bombs over most of the districts, but also on the Dunes marshalling yards, the port and, once again, the Saint-Pol refinery whose fuel tanks had been on fire for ten days and which would continue to burn for some time to come. Malo-les-Bains and Rosendaël were also hit. There were so many killed that coffins soon ran out and the bodies had to be buried in mass graves.

Bastion 32 seen here at the beginning of the 21st century. It is now home to an Operation Dynamo museum. (Erik Groult-Heimdal.)

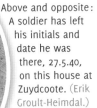

Above and opposite: A soldier has left his initials and date he was there, 27.5.40, on this house at Zuydcoote. (Erik Groult-Heimdal.)

Minck square in the town centre after an air raid. (Archives de Dunkerque – CMUA.)

This unprecedented attack did not spare ships arriving in Dunkirk or trying to leave. Around ten civilian or military ships were hit or sunk, including the French freighter *Monique Schiaffino* berthed on the quayside and whose burning fuel spread across the basin, setting fire to another freighter, the *Aden*.

Despite everything, the evacuation continued throughout the day, but it was far from going as planned. Due to the intensity of the air raids, the hospital ships trying to get into the port had to turn back. Also, the operations on the beaches were proving to be desperately slow. Indeed, precious time was lost in the slow return trips with rowboats and lifeboats transporting soldiers from the sands to the large ships anchored a relatively long way off the shore due to the region's very gently sloping sands.

The Belgian army surrendered on 28 May, dangerously opening up the left flank of the British Expeditionary Force. Seen here is a Belgian column that has just surrendered (as seen by the white flags on the trucks), passing a German horse-drawn column. (archives Heimdal.)

Abandoned British trucks in Dunkirk. As more and more vehicles arrived with the withdrawing troops, the order was given to stop any more from entering the bridgehead perimeter. (BA.)

In these conditions, only 7,669 soldiers were embarked by the end of this first full day of Operation Dynamo. This was a long way off what Rear-Admiral Ramsey had planned for, that is to say 45,000 men per day.

Tuesday 28 May

The Germans did not wait long to take advantage of the Belgian surrender in vigour since daybreak. Their general staff's objective was to now cut the French 1st army in two, thus cutting off the seven divisions concentrated around Lille and reaching Dunkirk as fast as possible.

The unfavourable evolution of the situation to the east of the front, and in the Lille sector, led Lord Gort to make the decision to pull back, as soon as possible, his units present on the Lys along the Poperinge-Ypres line. General Blanchard requested that the British Expeditionary Force commander delay the withdrawal by 24 hours, explaining that this was the only chance left to save his divisions defending Lille. Lord Gort refused, stating his government's *"explicit order to subordinate everything to the salvation of the expeditionary force."*

Lord Gort's attitude led to a serious deterioration in his dealings with the 1st army group commander, but also with general Prioux whose 1st army was under serious threat with its northeast flank now in the air following the surrender of the Belgian army. However, nothing could change the British decision to pull out. By the end of the day, the four BEF divisions concerned by Gort's order were withdrawn, as planned, north of the Lys.

In the Dunkirk sector, towards which a growing number of British and French soldiers were converging, the evacuation continued in the same difficult conditions, despite the fact that the rain, which began falling at the start of the afternoon over the town, prevented a new air raid.

After having destroyed their materiel and vehicles, the first three divisions to be withdrawn, the 1st, 4th and 46th Divisions, boarded ships from the beaches of Zuydcoote and La Panne, where Gort had transferred his HQ in the former villa of the Belgian king, Albert 1st. These units left France under the intense fire of the *Luftwaffe*, with Messerschmitt 109 fighters supporting the Stukas by strafing the beaches at low altitude.

As with the previous day, several ships were hit, either by planes or *Schnellboote*, or artillery batteries now able to reach Dunkirk. The cross channel steamer, *Queen of the Channel*, sank with 920 men on board, the survivors being picked up by another British ship, the *Dorrian Rose*.

Given the state of the port and the problems posed by evacuating off the beaches, Captain William Tennant, tasked by the Admiralty with organizing the evacuation on the ground,

British soldiers wait in the dunes for their turn to embark. They had to fight against fatigue, hunger, thirst and the threat of German planes. (IWM.)

decided to try and moor ships on the East Mole. Despite the latter not being made for this, the first attempt proved successful. From now on, this narrow 1,200-metre long plank causeway, barely able to take three men abreast and bordered on each side by a wooden plank, would see a succession of Royal Navy ships, notably destroyers, which embarked several hundred men at a time despite not being designed to transport troops.

Another favourable element arrived in the afternoon; the small boats of all shapes and sizes that had been gathered from all over Britain and taken to Dover to support Operation Dynamo. There were trawlers, barges, yachts, paddle steamers and even smaller craft that were tied together in a line and towed by tugs. This hotch-potch armada also comprised of thirty Dutch coasters that had escaped the German occupation, as well as French trawlers sent by rear-admiral Landriau, tasked by admiral Abrial with giving France's support to Dynamo, but

also the organisation of the evacuation of his own soldiers who were withdrawing to Dunkirk in increasing numbers.

On the evening of 28 May, 17,804 men had been evacuated from Dunkirk. This was still less than planned, but better than the previous day.

Above: A line of small boats is pulled by a tug which will take them to the Dunkirk Pocket in order to speed up the embarkation of soldiers. (IWM.)

The beach at Zuydcoote seen from the sanitarium. Soldiers await the small boats that will take them to the large ships anchored offshore, others await their turn, sitting or laying on the sand. (Private collection.)

Opposite and below: British soldiers crammed onto the decks of ships leaving for Britain. Although most faces express relief, others appear exhausted by what they have just lived through. (IWM.) (Archives de Dunkerque – CMUA.)

British soldiers walking along the beach at Dunkirk between beached ships and the corpses of their brothers in arms. (Archives de Dunkerque – CMUA.)

The barn was rebuilt in 2000 on the site of "La Plaine du Bois" and has become a place of remembrance. (copyright Mairie d'Esquelbecq.)

Eighty-Four British prisoners massacred at Esquelbecq

On Tuesday 28 May, the Germans attacked the road junction of Wormhoudt on their advance to the sea (20 km south of Dunkirk), a strategic area staunchly defended by British forces lacking in ammunition and armoured support.

During the course of the fighting, a hundred soldiers of the Royal Warwickshire Regiment, Cheshire Regiment and Royal Artillery, were taken prisoner by elements of the 1st SS armoured division *Leibstandarte SS Adolf Hitler* and locked in a barn in a field known as the "La Plaine du Bois" situated in the neighbouring village of Esquelbecq.

Flouting the Geneva Convention, the *Waffen-SS* threw stick grenades into the barn, killing and wounding many of the men inside. The survivors were shot outside and inside the barn, but a few managed to get away. Some were picked up a few days later by the *Wehrmacht* and given medical treatment before being sent to POW camps. In all, eighty-four men were killed on 28 May at "La Plaine du Bois".

After the war, the site of the massacre became a place of remembrance. The barn was rebuilt as it looked in 1940 and eighty-four plane trees planted on the path leading to the site. A memorial was also placed nearby recalling the deaths of three hundred military personnel and civilians around the villages of Wormhoudt, Ledringhem and Esquelbecq during the tragic days of the spring of 1940.

Wednesday 29 May

During the morning of 29 May, the German forces advancing from the west linked up in front of the *Monts des Flandres* with those from the east, thirty kilometres from the sea. This meant that the elements of the French 1st army remaining behind the Lys were now cut off. General Prioux, who had taken over from general Blanchard three days earlier as commander of the 1st army, was captured along with his headquarters staff.

The German link up marked the start of the siege of the Dunkirk Pocket which was shrinking rapidly, despite the resistance of its defenders; the British to the east and the French to the west. All this was taking place with an ever increasing flow of military personnel into the shrinking perimeter. The mass arrival of French troops led to a sorting station being set up east of Bray-Dunes, some three kilometres in length along the seafront and divided up into unit regrouping zones.

Throughout the whole day, the evacuation operations continued in extremely difficult conditions. With a clear sky, the *Luftwaffe* went back on the attack, with the Messerschmitt 109 fighters ensuring air superiority whilst successive waves of Stukas attacked the port, beaches and shipping. The men on land, and at sea, experienced total hell. Olivier Bocher, a quarter-master on board the destroyer *Sirocco*, which was attacked in the afternoon, wrote the following vivid account: *"All around us was a veritable hail of bombs and fire. The Stukas dive bombed us with their screeching sirens loud enough to burst our eardrums. One had to have nerves of steel to not go mad in this storm of steel and fire. The anti-aircraft guns of the ships opened a steady fire on the planes. Several of them were shot down (...). Close to us, a destroyer, trawler and a troopship were hit by bombs. The trawler sank within seconds. (...) Around us was nothing but desolation. Men swam in a sea turned red with blood; it became black with fuel which spread across the surface. And amongst all this carnage, the embarkation of troops continued (...)."* [1] The *Sirocco* managed to sail to Dover in the early hours of the night with almost 600 soldiers on board.

On this Wednesday, many ships taking part in Operation Dynamo were sunk, bombed or hit by torpedoes fired by the *Schnellboote*. The paddle steamer, *Crested Eagle*, was attacked by Stukas as it left the port after having picked up the survivors of a troopship sunk in one of the basins. On fire, it managed to reach the coast at Zuydcoote. Many of the people on board were burned alive on the deck. The survivors jumped into the sea, but were strafed by *Luftwaffe* planes. It is estimated that three hundred of the six hundred men on board the *Crested Eagle* were killed (see annex page 76).

The Royal Navy lost several ships including the destroyers, *HMS Wakeful*, cut in half by a

Quarter-master Olivier Bocher, a crew member of the *Sirocco*. (archives Heimdal.)

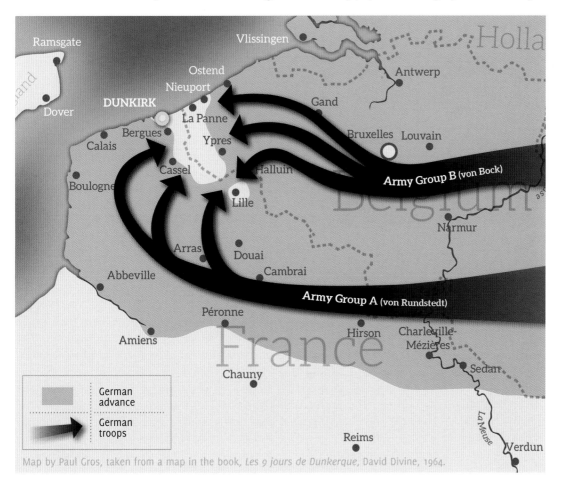

German advance

German troops

Map by Paul Cros, taken from a map in the book, *Les 9 jours de Dunkerque*, David Divine, 1964.

The German advance by 29 May 1940. Army groups A and B linked up north-west of Lille, cutting off the men defending the city from the rest of the pocket.

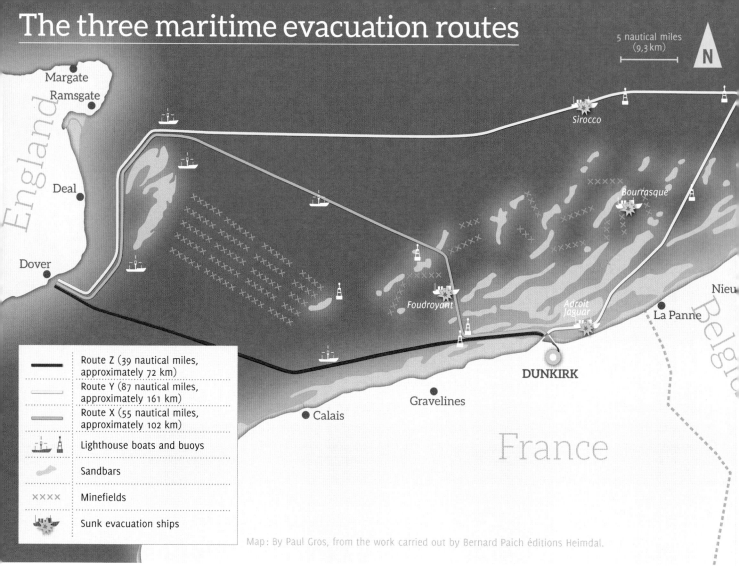

5 nautical miles
(9,3 km)

N

	Route Z (39 nautical miles, approximately 72 km)
	Route Y (87 nautical miles, approximately 161 km)
	Route X (55 nautical miles, approximately 102 km)
	Lighthouse boats and buoys
	Sandbars
××××	Minefields
	Sunk evacuation ships

Map: By Paul Gros, from the work carried out by Bernard Paich éditions Heimdal.

torpedo, and *HMS Grafton*, hit by two torpedoes. Losses on both these ships were very high. The passenger steamer, *Mona's Queen*, transporting hundreds of drinking water containers for the men at Dunkirk, hit a mine and sank in less than two minutes along with most of its crew.

It would take too long to mention all of the ships lost or damaged on this day. At this rate, it was Operation Dynamo itself could soon be under threat. But what could be done to try and stop this massacre, with the *Luftwaffe*, *Kriegsmarine* and artillery on land all constantly firing at the Dunkirk Pocket?

The British Admiralty decided to get as many men as possible off the beaches as the port was mostly unusable. Also, the East Mole had become a prime target for the German pilots due to the amount of ships massed there. It was also decided to leave Route Z which was the shortest of the three routes, but also the most dangerous as it was exposed to enemy artillery fire from batteries set up on the high ground above Calais. The preferred route was now X (100 km) and Y (160 km), although the latter was nevertheless exposed to the danger of *Schnellboote* operating from Holland.

Despite the increasingly critical conditions, 47,310 men were evacuated on 29 May, some 30,000 more than the previous day.

Thursday 30 May

In the morning, the last survivors of the French 1st army entered the Dunkirk Pocket. They left behind them an impressive amount of materiel, with the pistol-brandishing British sentries forbidding any vehicles or heavy weapons from entering the perimeter. This measure was not without creating tension between the two allies, notably with some officers of the mechanised units.

Some three-hundred thousand British and French troops were now closed in a pocket measuring thirty kilometres in length and ten wide, bordered to the west by the Mardyke canal, to the south by the Colme canal and which continued to the east as far as Nieuport. The only way out was via the sea, which brought hope, but also death.

General Falgade, tasked by admiral Abrial with the defence of the bridgehead, could count on two newly arrived French units to strengthen the 60th infantry division units, the Flanders fortified sector units and the 68th infantry division, exhausted by several days of fighting. The two new units were the 12th mechanised infantry division led by general Janssen, and the 32nd infantry division commanded by general Lucas. Despite also being understrength and worn down by fighting, these two divisions had retained operational capabilities and they would prove so throughout the following days.

Inside the pocket, the situation was becoming increasingly confused. Columns of French soldiers appeared from everywhere, making their way to the dunes and beach, bunched together in conditions that were made worse by the heat. As for food supplies, it was every man for himself. Rations were taken from abandoned British trucks and where there was nothing, stray horses were shot for food. With the breakdown in supply services, it was left to the men to organise their own cooking, as described by the Dunkirk veteran and writer, Robert Merle, in his post-war novel, Week-end à Zuydcoote (see annex page 82). In order to supply the thousands of hungry, dehydrated and exhausted men, the British beached barges loaded with water and food at high tide.

In the general chaos, some French soldiers who had lost their units tried to enter British embarkation zones where they were refused entry, sometimes at the point of a gun, creating tension between the two allies. In an attempt to improve the situation, both staffs agreed on the dividing up of the beaches, with a possible modification in favour of the French as the British

Above: 30 May. *HMS Vanquisher*, berthed along the East Mole in the port of Dunkirk, finished loading her contingent of soldiers. Embarkation was carried out in tricky conditions as the mole was not designed for berthing ships. Makeshift ladders and gangways had to be used depending on the tides. (IWM.)

Opposite: *HMS Vanquisher* leaves Dunkirk, leaving behind a town in flames with the thick smoke rising high into the sky. (IWM.)

gradually departed. Personnel, recognisable by their green and white armbands, were tasked with regulating the flow of men and directing them to where they should go. Also, in Dover, a group was formed with the aim of coordinating naval means set up respectively by the British and the French. For the latter, this was the "*Flotille du Pas-de-Calais*" (Dover Straights Fleet) gathering together trawlers and other civilian ships, as well as naval ships.

At the beginning of the morning, hundreds of "little ships" reached beaches, following the call made by the authorities over the BBC wavelengths. They would allow for the speeding up of transferring men from the shore to ships anchored off the beaches. This was a resounding success with 53,823 men taken off during the day, more than the previous day, and including more than eight thousand Frenchmen.

However, for the latter, Thursday 30 May was also marked by the loss of the destroyer, *Bourrasque*. In mid-afternoon, after having taken on board eight hundred men from the Félix Faure quayside, it cast off, followed by another destroyer of the same class, the *Branlebas*. Shortly before 5pm, as she was sailing off Nieuport, the stern shook under the effects of a large explosion, seemingly caused by a magnetic mine. *"I ran out onto the deck that was covered in corpses, officers were trying to maintain order. The ship had been seriously damaged. It was already slowly settling into the water, listing to starboard. Panic-stricken soldiers were leaping into the water, still*

After having taken on more than a thousand men on the Félix Faure quayside, the destroyer, *Bourrasque*, cast off at around 3pm, followed by the destroyers *Bouclier* and the *Branlebas*. At around 4.15pm, as she was sailing off Nieuport, she hit a magnetic mine, severely damaging the stern. (Illustration by Erik Groult.)

wearing their haversacks and sank like stones. Orders were being shouted all over the place. The order given to gather on both sides of the ship to try and retain some balance went unheard", stated the young Dunkirk sailor, Louis Spitaels, who was one of the eight hundred on board. [(2)]

The *Branlebas* immediately stopped her engines and put down the lifeboats. Other survivors were picked up by British trawlers. Approximately five hundred men perished in this catastrophe.

Friday 31 May

As the sun rose over the beaches, the scene it lit up contrasted with that of the previous days. Thanks to the smooth running of the night evacuations, the wide swathes of sand appeared strangely empty. They were soon, however, filled with French soldiers who were arriving in ever-increasing numbers. The British Admiralty, answering Churchill's wishes,

decided that from now on, British and French soldiers should be embarked on an equal footing. On land, there were an increasing number of incidents concerning French soldiers cut off from their units, trying by all available means to board ships on the East Mole, with Royal Navy personnel sometimes pushing them away in a brutal manner. These scenes differed totally from the warm welcome reserved for the French when they arrived in England, with women providing them with cigarettes, sandwiches and drinks. They were also given wash items and clean clothing and schools were emptied in order to provide accommodation.

During the morning of 31 May, the heavy swell rendered the task of the "little ships" difficult, the latter being even more numerous than the previous day. The wind, clearing the mist and the smoke from the fires, allowed the German artillery and *Luftwaffe* to resume their attacks against the Dunkirk Pocket. However, the Royal Air Force hit back and shot down thirty

Shortly after the explosion, the destroyer began to sink by the stern. Men at the bow are leaping into the water. (ECPAD.)

Above and opposite: Following closely behind the *Bourrasque*, the *Branlebas* stopped her engines and put down the lifeboats to save the men on board the hit destroyer. A hundred others were picked up by two British trawlers, but five hundred men perished in the attack. (ECPAD.)

enemy aircraft. The Germans particularly targeted the makeshift jetties, made from lines of trucks which had speeded up embarkation. These low-altitude dogfights were watched with interest by the men gathered on the sands, as related by the writer Robert Merle, interviewed after the war for television. *"The blokes were laying in the dunes and watching the dogfights, applauding as if they were at a show. The situation was somewhat absurd and Kafkaesque. The weather was nice and at the same time, the Stukas were bombing, aiming for the boats and beaches."*

The threat also came from the *Kriegsmarine*. Difficult to make out from the armada of "little ships", the fast boats created devastation with their torpedoes. During the night, one of them hit the French *Bourrasque* class destroyer, *Sirocco*, as it headed to England. It was finished off by a Stuka, the bomb of which hit the hold containing ammunition for the 130 mm guns, cutting the ship in half. On board were 930 soldiers and sailors, including some of general Blanchard's staff officers; there were only 270 survivors.

Tensions between the British and the French were not only reserved for the embarkation operations. They were also felt at the highest echelons. Lord Gort, who had to leave for England during the day, wrote to admiral Abrial

informing him that he was leaving three BEF divisions to support the French in defending the Dunkirk Pocket until the end of the evacuation of French and British troops. However, his successor, Major-General Alexander, stated to Abrial and Falgade that his units: *"would be unable to hold the front, given their state of fatigue and lack of armaments due to the fighting they have just undertaken."* The new BEF commander added that Lord Gort had not tasked him with supporting French troops, but to withdraw as soon as all of the British troops had embarked.

As Lord Gort had already left and was, therefore, unable to explain the obviously contradictory orders, the French command could do nothing but take note of their ally's position. *"As it is no longer possible to count on English cooperation, the mission that I have been given will be carried out by French troops alone. We, the French, are tied to the imperative mission of holding out to the death in order to save as many personnel as possible in the Dunkirk bridgehead. As long as this objective has not been achieved, we will remain here"*, was the solemn reply from admiral Abrial to Maj. Gen. Alexander.

31 May marked the high point of Operation Dynamo, with the evacuation of 68,014 men, including 14,874 French.

Princess Elizabeth back to the site of its exploits

The *Princess Elizabeth* returned to Dunkirk in 1999 and can be seen in the port today. (Erik Groult-Heimdal.)

Her bright colours and strange outline never fails to draw attention. Berthed in the port opposite the "Pole Marine" shopping centre in the heart of the town of Dunkirk, the *Princess Elizabeth* took part in and witnessed Operation Dynamo. This paddle steamer was part of the fleet of "little ships" and made four crossings between France and England; the first three up to Bray-Dunes beach and the last to the East Mole at Dunkirk. In all, she took back around 1,700 soldiers, including 500 French.

Built in 1926 and thus named, following the tradition of the British navy, to celebrate the birth of George VI's daughter, this 59-metre long ship started out as a pleasure steamer along the south coast of England and as a ferry between Southampton and the Isle of Wight.

She was requisitioned in September 1939 as a Royal Navy minesweeper due to her shallow draft. The forward deck was equipped with a 105 mm gun. Based at Southampton with the code number J 111, she joined the 10th Minesweeping Flotilla of the Dover Patrol. After the events at Dunkirk, for which she was awarded the Dunkirk 1940 medal, she was equipped with anti-aircraft guns for the rest of the war.

The *Princess Elizabeth* carried out four crossings between England and France during Operation Dynamo. (Archives de Dunkerque – CMUA.)

After the war she went back to her coastal role and was fitted with diesel engines in 1946, becoming a pleasure boat between 1959 and 1965. She was then transformed into a floating casino, then a restaurant and pub berthed at a quay on the Thames in London. She was bought by the Paris Chambre syndicale typographique in 1987; berthed at the Javel quay and became an exhibition and conference centre.

Finally, in 1999, she was purchased by the town of Dunkirk as a centre for the town's big festive events. She was back to the site of her exploits following a long and full life. Even if there is little of origin left, apart from the rudder, paddle wheels and bulwarks, her presence in the rebuilt port both bears witness to the terrible events of the spring of 1940, and is a symbol of Franco-British friendship.

Saturday 1 June

Encircled for almost a week, out of ammunition and not knowing what to do with the numerous wounded, the some thirty-five thousand defenders of the Lille Pocket could not hold out for much longer. During the night, their commander, general Molinié, had signed the surrender document offered by the commander of *XXVII. Armeekorps*, general Waeger. In recognition of the bravery of the defeated men, the Germans rendered them military honours on the large square in Lille on the morning of Saturday 1 June. In his Second World War memoirs, Churchill also paid homage to the courage shown by the soldiers of the 1st army which had gained precious time for his expeditionary force: *"The epic resistance of Molinié without doubt allowed for the evacuation of a further one hundred thousand men from Dunkirk"*.

At the same time in Dunkirk, Major-General Alexander confirmed to admiral Abrial that he planned to leave France the following night with the last elements of the expeditionary force, leaving the defence of what was left of the Pocket to the French forces alone.

To the west, where the French 68th infantry division was positioned, with the 32nd infantry division in reserve, the German bombardments became heavier. They also increased in intensity against the southern part of the defence line, guarded by units of the Flanders fortified sector, where the German *18., 254.* and *14. Infanterie-Divisionen* were attacking. In the east, the 12th mechanised infantry division was now in the front line facing the *216.* and *56. Infanterie-Divisionen*. Everywhere, the French troops put up a ferocious defence against the Germans: *"Despite our overwhelming superiority in both numbers and materiel, the French counter-attacked in several areas. I cannot comprehend how these soldiers, fighting one against twenty, managed to find the strength to attack. It is stupefying. I see in these soldiers the same ardour as those of Verdun in 1916. We are unable to break through anywhere and suffer terrifying losses"* stated the *18. Armee* commander, general Georg von Küchler, in his war diary; his army having been tasked with closing down the Dunkirk Pocket.

The efficient resistance of the bridgehead defenders allowed the embarkation to continue at a fast rate throughout the day. This was done despite the continuous *Luftwaffe* attacks and the increasingly accurate artillery fire. On 1 June, German planes launched their heaviest attack since the start of Operation Dynamo. The entire coastline was targeted from Dunkirk to La Panne, but also the anti-aircraft positions south of Bray-Dunes, the port, train station and the

Opposite and below: A ceremony organised on 1 June, the day after the surrender of Lille. These parading French soldiers are saluted by the Germans. This was a chivalrous way for the victors to pay homage to the bravery of the defeated. (BA.)

town where many civilians were killed. Ships were also hit at sea.

In the space of a few hours, the Stukas sunk four Royal Navy destroyers, as well as two of the biggest cross channel ferries. The French destroyer, *Foudroyant*, *"surrounded by a swarm of Stukas"* according to a report, was sunk as she tried to enter the port.

Admiral Ramsey sent more ships to Dunkirk so that the evacuation could continue throughout the night. The total of men evacuated on 1 June was 64,429, of which 35,013 were French. 32,248 were taken by French ships, a figure which shows the increasing efficiency of the *"Flotille du Pas-de-Calais"*, that had been rapidly put together by admiral Landriau.

Above: La Panne (Belgium), 1 June. The corpse of a British corporal of the 4th Infantry Division, lies at the foot of a vehicle. (BA.)

Below: Throughout the day of 1 June, many British and French ships fell victim to German air attacks. Seen here are survivors from *SS Mona's Queen* heading towards *HMS Vanquisher*. (IWM.)

Above: These British soldiers have no choice but to wade up to their shoulders in order to reach a shallow draft ship, anchored relatively close to the beach. (IWM.)

Below: These French soldiers gathered around Bastion 32 reveal the increasing confusion at Dunkirk in the last days of Operation Dynamo. (Archives de Dunkerque – CMUA.)

Sunday 2 June

As general Falgade's order was to continue resistance throughout the day along presently held positions, the three French divisions, already worn down in the defence of the Dunkirk Pocket, would fight non-stop all day against the seven German divisions tasked with closing down the pocket.

Spurred on by their officers, the soldiers threw their last strength into the battle. This is what one of them wrote in his diary: *"Dunkirk is nothing but flames. The enemy planes attack us relentlessly. Perhaps our last hour is not far off. But we hold on to allow the embarkation of the allied troops. We will hold on to the end, knowing full well that we will be the last to be withdrawn."*

To the west, held by the French 68th infantry division, an attack was launched by the *61. Infanterie-Division* in the Spycker corridor (ten kilometres from Dunkirk), the weak spot of the defence line. French resistance was so strong that the German infantry had to have tank support from the *9. Panzer-Division*.

The same resistance was put up south of the perimeter, the crucial point of the Dunkirk defences, where the units of the Flanders fortified

forces launched a night counter-attack to push out elements of the *18. Infanterie-Division* positioned north of the Basse-Colme canal and in order to upset preparations being made for the impending and, no doubt large-scale, offensive.

Fighting continued throughout the day in this sector, with heavy losses on both sides.

French troops wait patiently on the beach, hoping that a ship will take them to England too. (Archives de Dunkerque – CMUA.)

Divisional general Louis Janssen, commander of the 12th mechanised infantry division, was killed at the Dunes fort during the air attack of 2 June. He was replaced by the divisional artillery commander, colonel Blanchon. (Heimdal archives.)

After having been buried on the evening of 2 June in one the Dunes fort's ditches, general Janssen's body was transferred to the Leffrinckouke cemetery after the war (near Dunes fort), where he rests amongst his men. (Erik Groult-Heimdal.)

German ground troops could rely on the intervention of Stukas in the face of the determination of French units, notably the *7e GRDI* (infantry division reconnaissance group) and the *18e GRCA* (army corps reconnaissance group).

The fighting was especially fierce for the ruins of Bergues, where the defenders continued to hold on despite the bombardments. For the Germans, it took the joint effort of the *Luftwaffe* and their heavy artillery to open a breach in the ramparts in the early hours of the afternoon. This strategic position, only ten kilometres from Dunkirk, fell around 5pm.

As we can see, the battering attacks of the *18. Infanterie-Division* pushed the forces of the Flanders fortified sector to the south of the defensive perimeter. To the east, the 12th mechanised infantry division was hit by intense artillery preparation in the early afternoon, followed by air attacks which caused great damage at Bray-Dunes and totally destroying the village of Ghyvelde. Despite all this, the various units held fast, blocking the advance of the *56. Infanterie-Division* and the *14. Infanterie-Division*.

However, the 12th mechanised infantry division was hit hard at the end of the afternoon. An attack by Stukas on the Dunes fort, where the headquarters staff were based, killed many men, including the divisional commander, general Janssen (see annex page 80). Following Janssen's death, command was taken over by the head of the divisional artillery, colonel Blanchon.

Inside the pocket, the evacuations continued. In the port, they became more and more difficult due to the shipwrecks and strong currents caused by the destruction of the locks. However, it was on the beaches that the situation was the most confused. Whereas the British were finishing their embarkations, there was a certain disorder with the French, of whom there were still fifty to sixty thousand not yet evacuated. Due to a lack of coordination between the French and the British, arriving detachments could not be embarked due to a lack of ships, whereas other ships were leaving virtually empty because the detachments were not arriving fast enough. It is estimated that ten thousand places were thus lost on this day.

The evacuation figures for 2 June were 26,256 men, of which 16,049 were French. At 11.30pm, Captain Tennant sent the following message to Rear-admiral Ramsey: *"BEF evacuated!"* The last batch of British troops were due to leave the next day and it had been agreed that the wounded being treated at the Zuydcoote and Rosendaël hospitals would not be taken. This painful decision was taken due to the numerous German attacks on hospital ships since the start of Operation Dynamo.

A *216. Infanterie-Division* infantryman seen here on 3 June near the village of Moëres. (ECPAD.)

Monday 3 June

The Germans resumed the offensive as soon as the sun rose. To the east of the pocket, and after an intense artillery barrage, the men of the *61. Infanterie-Division* attacked from Spycker that they had managed to take at the end of the previous day, but without being able to advance any further. Their objective was the crossing of the Bourbourg canal, the final obstacle before Dunkirk. François de Lannoy explained that: *"Once over the canal, they would be able to break through into the sectors of Saint-Pol and Petite-Synthe, go around Dunkirk from the west and reach directly the embarkation areas of the outer harbour and moles."* [3]

Like the previous day, it was the southern sector that was the most threatened. The Germans were only four kilometres from the Furnes canal, the last rampart before Dunkirk and its port. General Falgade therefore ordered the commander of the Flanders fortified sector to hold on another day and prevent the enemy from crossing the canal so that the evacuation could continue. The *18. Infanterie-Division* would, therefore, use all it could to overcome the French defences. With artillery and air support, the infantry attacked towards Coudekerque-Branche and Teteghem. Fighting raged on throughout the day, with the French defending each house in the same way the Soviets would at Stalingrad in the winter of 1942. By nightfall, the Germans had not managed to cross the Furnes canal at any point, behind

which the Flanders fortified sector forces had pulled back.

The enemy pressure was also felt in the east as soon as day broke, mostly between Ghyvelde and Uxem. The 12th mechanised infantry division units would resist throughout the entire day, but also at the cost of heavy losses, notably for the 8th Zouaves, 150th infantry regiment and the 92nd infantry division reconnaissance group. In this part of the front line, this day was marked by a new attack on the Dunes fort, the day after one which had cost the life of general Janssen. The Stukas returned late afternoon, their bombs killing several dozen men and destroying numerous vehicles parked near the fort.

At Dunkirk, the French headquarters staff were preparing the final phase of the evacuation. At 3pm, general Abrial informed the Admiralty that: *"The enemy is in the Dunkirk suburbs."* Early evening, after having burnt all the documents and destroyed the equipment, the commander of the North maritime forces left Bastion 32 for the last time. After having inspected the various embarkation areas, he embarked on a fast ship, along with general Falgade, for England.

Thousands of French soldiers who could not be evacuated in the destroyed port of Dunkirk. (ECPAD.)

Aerial view of the Texier lock and naval shipbuilding yards at the end of Operation Dynamo. Shipwrecks line the coast. (Archives de Dunkerque – CMUA.)

Under the protection of a few elements that remained in the line, in order to form a last protective "crust", the 68th infantry division, Flanders fortified sector forces and the 12th mechanised infantry division pulled back in a disciplined fashion after having destroyed their materiel and ammunition. These three big units could withdraw with honour; they had held on to the end. The enemy had never broken through their front lines, even if he was now less than five kilometres from the East Mole.

The Royal Navy and the French navy joined together in a final effort to send as many ships as possible to Dunkirk. There were more than sixty ships, with torpedo boats, destroyers and even fishing boats, as well as passenger ships, dredgers, corvettes and trawlers.

The first ships arrived at 10.30pm. It was planned to finish the bulk of the evacuations at 3.30am so that the ships could make for sea before day broke at around 5am at that time of year. Contrary to the previous days, the *Luftwaffe* was absent from the skies and artillery fire was weak. This can attributed, no doubt, to the fact that the Germans did not want to take the risk of firing on their own men who were now close to the port.

All of this was to the advantage to the embarkations, which began in rather favourable conditions.

However, from midnight onwards, hordes of French soldiers, cut off from their units, began to converge towards the East Mole, the sheer number and indiscipline of whom hindered the smooth running of operations. The consequence

of this was that many of the men of the 12th mechanised infantry division (12e DIM), the Flanders fortified sector forces (S.F.F.) and 68th infantry division (12e DI) were unable to embark.

The last ship to berth was the destroyer *HMS Shikari*, which cast off at 3.45am carrying six hundred S.F.F. Men.

Left on the quaysides were approximately forty thousand men, most of whom were part of the units which had defended the Dunkirk Pocket to the very end.

(1) An account quoted by François de Lannoy in his book, *Dunkerque 1940*, Heimdal, 2004.

(2) Account taken from the *Nord-Maritime* newspaper, 29 September 1942.

(3) François de Lannoy, *Dunkerque 1940*, Heimdal 2004.

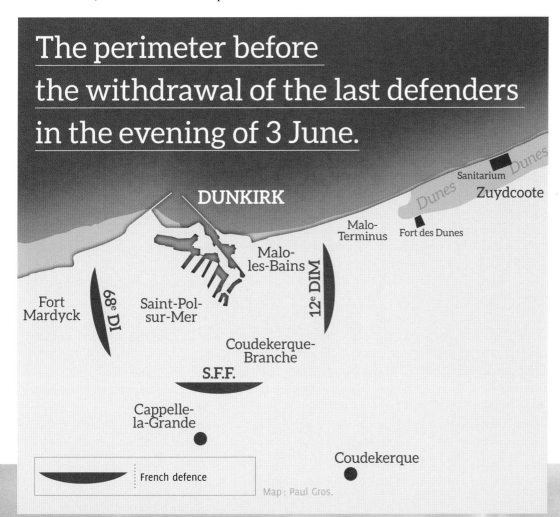

The perimeter before the withdrawal of the last defenders in the evening of 3 June.

DUNKIRK

Sanitarium

Dunes

Zuydcoote

Malo-Terminus

Fort des Dunes

Malo-les-Bains

12e DIM

Fort Mardyck

68e DI

Saint-Pol-sur-Mer

Coudekerque-Branche

S.F.F.

Cappelle-la-Grande

Coudekerque

French defence

Map: Paul Gros.

Below: The beach at Dunkirk today with the East Mole and port installations in the background. (Erik Groult-Heimdal.)

The Sanitarium farm today.
(Erik Groult-Heimdal.)

The Zuydcoote sanitarium in the heart of the battle

The imposing red-brick sanitarium of Dunkirk was a major element in the Battle of Dunkirk and Operation Dynamo. Built on the edge of the dunes, it housed, in 1940, five hundred town-dwelling children suffering from tuberculosis.

From 10 May onwards, it first took in wounded from Maubeuge and Arras, then those of Belgium and finally the majority of those from Dunkirk as the local hospital was soon overwhelmed due to the increasing air raids on the town and port.

On 22 May, all of the surviving medical units of the French 1st army set up there with their vehicles and equipment. Over the following days, the sanitarium would play an increasingly important role. Three surgical teams took it in turns to work in eight operating theatres.

During the worst of the fighting, the triage room constantly held between seven hundred

and a thousand wounded. The influx of air raid victims and the combat wounded was such that every floor of the huge building was filled from top to bottom. Even this was not enough and tents had to be erected in the grounds. Civilian and military personnel worked virtually non-stop, assisted by nuns from the Convent of the Infant Jesus. The less seriously wounded were transported to ships crossing to England and back.

Approximately twelve thousand French, British and German wounded were treated at the Zuydcoote sanitarium and around a thousand died there as a result of their wounds, or due to the bombardments that took place there. Indeed, from the end of May onwards, the approaching Germans attacked the buildings several times from the air and with artillery, despite the presence of huge red crosses painted on the roofs.

Due to the need to bury bodies left at the entrance, the decision was taken to create a burial

This cemetery was established in the dunes between the sanitarium and the northern farm. A thousand soldiers were buried there, but also some civilians, killed during Operation Dynamo. The cemetery was moved in 1953. (Photo M. Broutin.)

ground between the railway line and the staff accommodation area. A census of the bodies buried there was carried out in 1948, resulting in the figure of 130 British, eight Belgians, three Spanish, one Dutch and 794 French.

After the war, if families so desired, they could have the body of a relative exhumed and taken to a civilian cemetery of their choice. In 1953, the remaining 281 bodies were transferred to the new military cemetery created by the town for those that died during Operation Dynamo and gathering together the dead of several communities in the Dunkirk region.

Although the only original part of the building is the central area (the wings having been rebuilt), shell splinter damage from spring 1940 can be seen on the walls of the north farm, the buildings of which, after 21 May, housed the main French infirmary.

More than eighty years after Operation Dynamo, the establishment is still in use under the name of the Zuydcoote maritime hospital.

Battle damage from Operation Dynamo is still visible on the walls.
(Erik Groult-Heimdal.)

Zuydcoote beach seen from the fence of the sanitarium.
(Private collection.)

Junkers Ju 87 B "Stuka", *Luftwaffe* 4th squadron, 77th dive-bomber wing (*Sturzkampfgeschwader 77*), abbreviation: 4./St.G77.
The "Stuka" is the most famous Second World War dive-bomber. It is the emblematic plane of the Battle of France, bringing panic to civilians with its screeching sirens and playing an important role in shattering successive allied, French and British counter-attacks against the advancing German armoured divisions. The survivors of Dunkirk did not forget its destructive attacks against ships loaded with soldiers trying to reach England. (Profile by Thierry Vallet.)

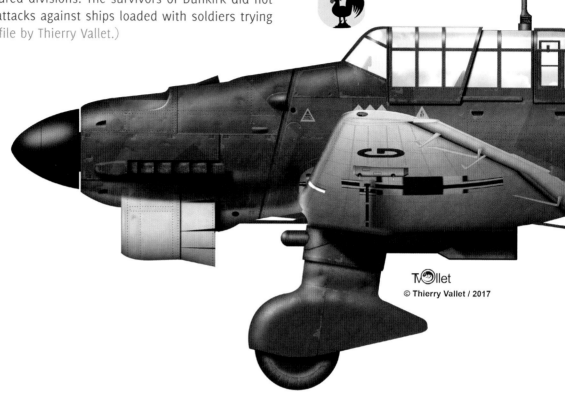

© Thierry Vallet / 2017

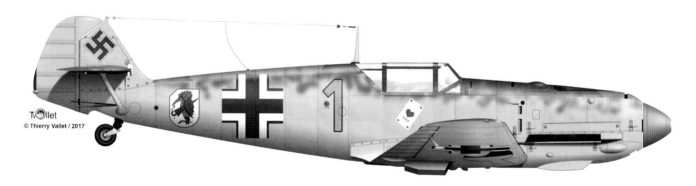

© Thierry Vallet / 2017

Messerschmitt Bf 109 E, *Luftwaffe* 6th squadron, 51st fighter wing (*Jagdgeschwader 51*), abbreviation: 6./J6 51. This plane was flown by *Oberleutnant* Josef Priller, nicknamed "Pips" by his comrades, born in Ingolstadt, 25 July 1915. Promoted to *Staffelkapitän* (squadron leader) of the 6./J6 51 in September 1939, Priller shot down a Spitfire and a Hurricane in the skies over Dunkirk.
Almost four years later, day for day, after Operation Dynamo, Josef Priller would go down in history, along with his wingman, Heinz Wodarczyk, as the first German pilot to go into action over the landing beaches on 6 June 1944. This can be seen in the 1962 film 'The Longest Day'. Priller never got to see the film as he died of a heart attack on 20 May 1961 at the age of 45. He achieved a tally of 101 aerial victories during the war. (Profile by Thierry Vallet.)

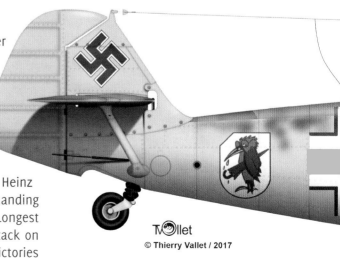

© Thierry Vallet / 2017

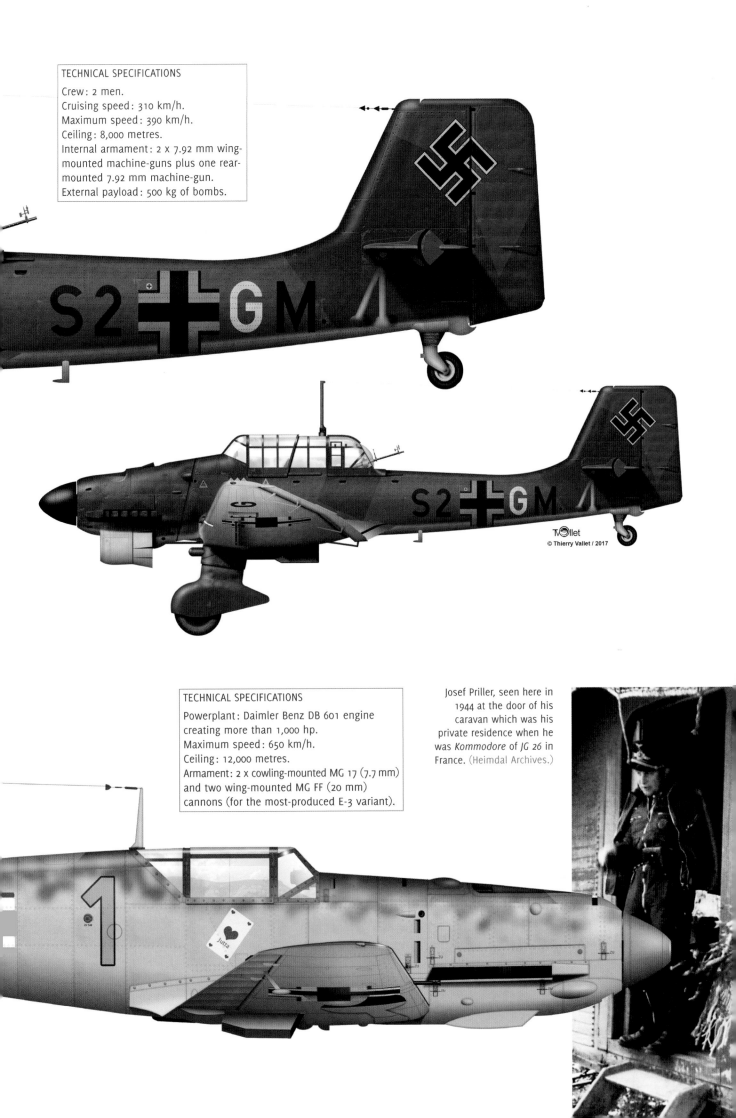

TECHNICAL SPECIFICATIONS

Crew: 2 men.
Cruising speed: 310 km/h.
Maximum speed: 390 km/h.
Ceiling: 8,000 metres.
Internal armament: 2 x 7.92 mm wing-mounted machine-guns plus one rear-mounted 7.92 mm machine-gun.
External payload: 500 kg of bombs.

TECHNICAL SPECIFICATIONS

Powerplant: Daimler Benz DB 601 engine creating more than 1,000 hp.
Maximum speed: 650 km/h.
Ceiling: 12,000 metres.
Armament: 2 x cowling-mounted MG 17 (7.7 mm) and two wing-mounted MG FF (20 mm) cannons (for the most-produced E-3 variant).

Josef Priller, seen here in 1944 at the door of his caravan which was his private residence when he was *Kommodore* of *JG 26* in France. (Heimdal Archives.)

© Thierry Vallet / 2017

Hurricane Mk.I code P2994, Royal Air Force 605 Squadron based at Hawkinge, Kent. The squadron's insignia was a standing bear painted on the tail fin.

The Hurricane was the first British monoplane and entered into service in December 1937. Contrary to the Spitfire, which appeared only a few months after, it barely evolved throughout its service life.

Despite heavy losses during the Battle of France, the Hurricane succeeded in destroying twice as many German planes. Along with the Spitfire, they would play an important role in protecting all sorts of ships taking part in Operation Dynamo.

(Profile by Thierry Vallet.)

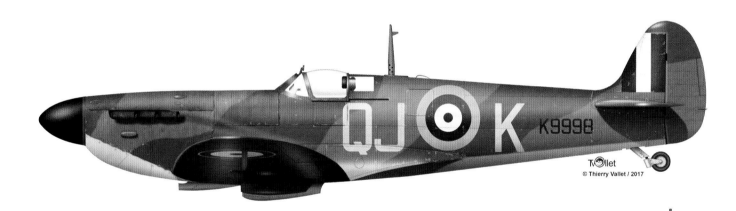

Supermarine Spitfire Mk.I code K9998, Royal Air Force 92 Squadron based at Hornchurch, Essex. It was flown by Flying Officer Geoffrey Wellum, DFC. The Supermarine Spitfire entered into service in August 1938 and was one of the most-used RAF and allied planes during the Second World War. The number of variants had never been seen before in the field of aviation. Faster and more agile, pilots preferred the Spitfire over the Hurricane for attacking enemy fighters, giving the latter the role of attacking bombers due to its slower speed and robustness. It was the combination of these two aircraft that allowed the RAF to win the Battle of Britain. (Profile by Thierry Vallet.)

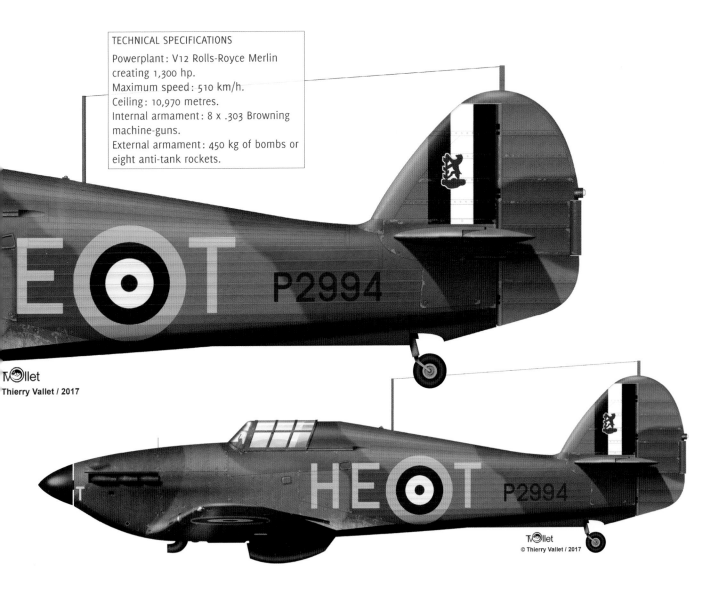

TECHNICAL SPECIFICATIONS

Powerplant: V12 Rolls-Royce Merlin creating 1,300 hp.
Maximum speed: 510 km/h.
Ceiling: 10,970 metres.
Internal armament: 8 x .303 Browning machine-guns.
External armament: 450 kg of bombs or eight anti-tank rockets.

TECHNICAL SPECIFICATIONS

Powerplant: V12 Rolls-Royce Merlin creating 1,030 hp.
Maximum speed: 570 km/h.
Ceiling: 10,400 metres.
Armament: 8 x .303 Browning machine-guns.

Operation Dynamo, a success but not a victory

With the British Expeditionary Force evacuated, but without its materiel and heavy weaponry, and forty thousand French soldiers taken prisoner, it was a mixed outcome for the Allies. As for Dunkirk, with 90% of the town destroyed, the outcome was unquestionably dramatic.

A group of German soldiers on the beach strewn with all sorts of objects with, in the background, beached ships. On the right are the remains of a British camp, as seen by the flag which is still present. (Archives de Dunkerque-CMUA-Fonds Albert Chatelle.)

A group of German soldiers look at a line of trucks that had been used as a makeshift jetty. (IWM.)

When the sun rose over Dunkirk on Tuesday 4 June 1940, it revealed a surprising spectacle and one that was far-removed from that of the previous days. After two weeks of almost uninterrupted noise, a heavy silence fell across the town and port. The thick smoke, still pouring out of the St. Pol tanks, only added to the atmosphere.

There were a lot less men on the beaches, but thousands had crowded onto the moles and surrounding areas. For the most part, these were soldiers from the units that had defended the perimeter to the very end.

These soldiers, not knowing what to make of things and exhausted from the fighting and another sleepless night, looked across a desperately empty sea from where their salvation should

have come. Realising that no other boats were going to come, some of them moved back to the beaches, either from fear of further *Luftwaffe* attacks, or in order to look for a boat that they could make seaworthy. Others tried to get to Calais via the coast but they were soon captured.

Some attempts, however, succeeded. A group of non-commissioned officers from the 7th and 92nd infantry divisions reconnaissance groups managed to reach England on a small trawler named *Irma Maria*. Other French soldiers found salvation on board the *Alcyon*, a small motor fishing boat, or the *Maude*, a sail fishing boat that took sixteen hours to reach England.

The first German patrols entered the town at around 8am. After meeting with the mayor, Auguste Waeteraere, at the town hall, the commander of the 68th infantry division, general Beaufrere, established contact with the Germans as he was the superior officer to have held that rank for the longest time. At around 10am, he went by car to Malo-les-Bains where he met the general commanding the *18. Infanterie-Division*.

This spelled the end of all resistance in Dunkirk. The Swastika flag was raised over the town hall. During the course of the morning, the forty thousand or so prisoners were gathered together in a temporary camp set up along the bastion walls between Dunkirk and Malo. Within a few days they would begin the journey to Germany and years of captivity.

Between 26 May and the very first hours of 4 June, 338,226 men [1] had been evacuated from the Dunkirk Pocket, including 125,000 French and 16,000 Belgian and Dutch soldiers. For the ships, the cost had been high. Out of the approximately 850 ships of all tonnage, British, French and others, which had taken part in Operation Dynamo, almost 240 had been sunk or

The forty thousand or so men taken prisoner during the morning of 4 June were mostly from the French units that had defended the perimeter to the very end. (Heimdal Archives.)

resulted in preventing the *Luftwaffe* from stopping the evacuation by inflicting heavy losses against them. *Generalfeldmarschall* Kesselring, commander of *Luftflotte 2*, tasked with wiping out the northern armies and Dunkirk, alongside *Luftflotte 3*, stated that *"These operations had exhausted our men and materiel, and reduced our forces to 30 and 50% of their strength."*

According to the British historian, David Divine, the RAF lost a hundred aircraft during Operation Dynamo, and the *Luftwaffe* around 130, but here too we should state that some German aircraft were shot down by British or French anti-aircraft guns.

Dynamo had allowed Britain to save all of its expeditionary force. This was unquestionably a strategic success in itself as these were its best units made up of professional soldiers led by skilled officers. However, the BEF had to abandon all of its heavy materiel: 2,500 guns, 75,000 motor vehicles, 11,000 machine-guns, to which was added 76,000 tonnes of munitions and 600,000 tonnes of fuel and supplies.

Of course, it would take time to replenish the stocks but, as many historian agree today, Great Britain could not have continued the war with as much efficiency, from North Africa to Germany, via Normandy, if it had left its BEF in France.

In this, Churchill was proved right by history, on 4 June before the House of Commons, rejoicing in the deliverance of *"The whole root and core and brain of the British Army, on which and around which we were to build, and are to build, the great British Armies in the later years of the war"*. *"Wars are not won by evacuations.*

damaged. The French navy had lost fifty of its ships engaged, including two destroyers and five torpedo ships. The Royal Navy had also been hit hard with six destroyers sunk and twenty-three others damaged.

As the rest of the war would show, these heavy naval losses proved the great vulnerability of surface ships, equipped with weak anti-aircraft defences, against modern land-based aviation. And yet, the Royal Air Force had put up a creditable performance, something that is forgotten too often when one speaks of events at Dunkirk, especially as they were the theatre of the first major confrontation between the RAF and the *Luftwaffe*, one month before the Battle of Britain.

Although they had not been able to clear the skies of the German fighters and bombers, the numerous sorties flown by the British pilots

The morning of 4 June. German infantrymen grab some rest in a Dunkirk street. Despite their fatigue, they bear the smile of victors. (BA.)

French prisoners wearing all sorts of attire, have attracted the attention of German photographers. (BA.)

But there was a victory inside this deliverance, which should be noted." Stated the British Prime Minister. Lt.General Alan Brooke, a key player in Operation Dynamo, echoed similar sentiments when he stated that *"It is difficult to see how Britain could have carried on the war without Dunkirk."* He would later go on to play a vital role in preparations for the Normandy landings.

As for the French, the result should be looked at on two levels. The various divisions played, to the very end, a major role in the success of the evacuation, carrying out decisive rearguard actions, notably at Boulogne, Calais and Lille and holding the Dunkirk defensive perimeter to the very end.

However, from a strategic point of view, for the French army, Dunkirk was the beginning of the end, losing in three weeks of fighting, no less

Above: Somewhere in Dunkirk, a dead French soldier lays amongst litter and abandoned items of equipment. (BA.)

These French soldiers, photographed by the Germans, had set up home in a Citroën bus and kitchen, seen on the left. (BA.)

than twenty-four infantry divisions and six motorised infantry divisions. Out of the 125,000 French soldiers evacuated from Dunkirk, almost 100,000 were sent back to France within several hours, or several days. Their role had been insignificant in the pursuit of the fighting and most would end up captured along with their leaders.

For the French army, Dunkirk was also the beginning of a collapse in morale and which would only increase up to the armistice on 22 June. And finally, Dunkirk greatly damaged the *Entente Cordiale*, which had begun in 1904 between the two "hereditary enemies". What followed was a reciprocal defiance which was not improved by the tragedy of Mers-el-Kébir a month later and which the Vichy government would exploit throughout four years.

As for the Germans, results were mixed. Of course, after Belgium and Holland, they had shown in northern France their tactical and materiel superiority. Indeed, we are tempted to write Panzer + Stukas, the winning combination. But although they put out of action 400,000 French soldiers between 10 May and 4 June, and had captured 40,000 at Dunkirk, they had not prevented the evacuation of the British Expeditionary Force, something that would cost them dearly later on. The American historian, Walter Lord stated that: *"The Battle of Dunkirk was a real turning point of the Second World War. With England beaten, Germany could have turned all of its forces towards Germany and Stalingrad would not have happened."* Guderian, the man behind the victory of the *Panzer-Divisionen* said the same thing when he summed up unambiguously that: *"Dunkirk was a catastrophe for Germany."*

On the other hand, for the town of Dunkirk and its inhabitants, there can be no debate. The town of Jean Bart had suffered 90% damage and was nothing but ruins following Operation Dynamo. Three thousand people had been killed and ten thousand wounded.

These Germans soldiers enjoy the seaside view across a beach that is still strewn with abandoned vehicles. (BA.)

After Operation Dynamo, the port was unusable due to the destruction and wrecked ships. (Archives de Dunkerque-CMUA-Fonds Albert Chatelle.)

In the town and on the beaches, the Germans discovered thousands of abandoned vehicles. (Archives de Dunkerque – CMUA.)

The beach of Malo-les-Bains, in front of the ruins of the casino, with the wreck of the *Adroit*. (Archives de Dunkerque – CMUA.)

Below: Jean Bart square after Operation Dynamo. (Archives de Dunkerque – CMUA.)

Its suffering was far from over. It would have to endure five long years of occupation. In a cruel twist of fate, it would experience another siege, from September 1944 to May 1945, with the German garrison only laying down its arms with the fall of the Nazi regime.

Even if most of its landmarks and dwellings had disappeared in the air raids, there remained of these tragic days of May and June 1940 a "Dunkirk Spirit", a symbol of resistance and fighting spirit which is still remembered on both sides of the Channel almost eighty years after.

(1) According to statistics drawn up by the British Admiralty.

Jean Bart square today. (Erik Groult-Heimdal.)

Dunkirk had suffered 90% destruction. The air raids had killed three thousand people and wounded ten thousand. (Archives de Dunkerque-CMUA-Fonds Albert Chatelle.)

Annex Reminders of Operation Dynamo, the shipwrecks

During low tides, the beaches at Dunkirk and those nearby, reveal barnacle-covered shapes. These are the remains of some of the two hundred or so allied ships of all types that were sunk in May and June 1940.

Although 338,000 British and French soldiers had been evacuated from the Dunkirk Pocket, many of the boats that had taken part in Operation Dynamo never reached their destinations. They were sunk by Stuka bombs or by mines, or became stuck in the sands only a few minutes after having set sail.

Many lay far out to sea between France and England but many sank near the port of Dunkirk and the beaches of Malo-les-Bains, Zuydcoote and Bray-Dunes. Today they are explored by divers looking for traces of the tragic events of May and June 1940 in the North Sea.

Even without putting on a diving suit and oxygen bottles, one can see the remains of some of the ships that took part in the biggest naval evacuation of all time. During the very low tides, the long beaches of Dunkirk and the surrounding area reveal metal carcasses eaten away by salt and covered with seaweed and barnacles.

There is not much left of the original ships and this is not just due to the passing years. Bruno Pruvost, a member of the Dunkirk diving club, who shares his passion for history and shipwrecks as a guide for the Flanders permanent centre for the environment, says that: *"All of the shipwrecks that could be reached were more or less broken up by the Germans for scrap metal. After the war, they were cut up again, this time down to the level of the sand. However, due to erosion, they are becoming increasingly visible."*

Bruno Pruvost takes people out to see these twisted skeletons and tells the story of each wreck. One of these stories is that of the *Crested Eagle*, visible on the beach at Zuydcoote. This 91-metre paddle steamer entered into service

The *Crested Eagle* was the first paddle steamer to sail on the Thames. She had a pivoting mast and telescopic funnel to allow for passage under the London bridges.
(Private collection.)

A German soldier has his photo taken on the the wreck of the *Crested Eagle*, beached off Zuydcoote during Operation Dynamo. (Private collection.)

in 1925 on the London-Ramsgate line. It was set on fire by Stuka bombs on 29 May 1940 off Malo-les-Bains just after having taken on board hundreds of British soldiers on the East Mole

Above: The *Crested Eagle* entered into service in 1925 on the London-Ramsgate line. 91 metres in length, this paddle steamer was one of the largest ships of its type. She was set on fire by Stuka bombs on 29 May 1940 off Malo-les-Bains, just after having taken soldiers on board. (Private collection.)

Opposite: At low tide, what remains of the *Crested Eagle* can be seen on the beach at Zuydcoote, where the ship beached in flames on 29 May 1940. (Erik Groult-Heimdal.)

at Dunkirk. Bruno Pruvost says that: *"The men on board were turned into human torches on the deck plates that had been heated by the fires below. Some of the men were scared to jump into the water, despite the shallow depth. Men floating on the surface were deliberately strafed. It is thought that 300 British soldiers lost their lives on this ship."*

A little further to the east, opposite the Bray-Dunes slipway, the inter-tidal zone reveals the remains of the *Devonia*, deliberately beached on 30 May 1940 whilst she was near La Panne in Belgium. This 75-metre long British paddle steamer, commissioned in 1905, was requisitioned at the outbreak of war and sent to Milford Haven to receive armaments and used as a minesweeper. Upon Operation Dynamo, she was with the Royal Navy's 6th Minesweeper Flotilla.

Now heading towards Dunkirk, one can see the remains of the *Claude*, to the west of the Zuydcoote sanitarium. This 32-metre long wooden flat-bottomed barge, towed across from England by a tug, was deliberately abandoned on the beach on 29 May 1940 following the unloading of her cargo of drinking water for the besieged men in the Dunkirk Pocket. The Claude was one of a series of two-hundred ships of the same type, the "X-Lighters", built in 1915 for unloading off large ships off the Turkish coast as part of the Dardanelles campaign. Five other "X-Lighters" took part in Operation Dynamo.

Opposite the slipway of Malo-Terminus on the beach of Dunkirk, can be seen the wreck of the *Lorina* at low tide. This 89-metre long English passenger ship had entered into service in December 1918, sailing between the pre-war crossing of Saint-Malo and the Channel Islands. Requisitioned by the Royal Navy on 11 September 1939 as a troopship, she sailed to Dover at the start of Operation Dynamo.

On 29 May 1940, she was off the beach at Dunkirk when an air attack broke the stern. The ship sank in shallow waters, despite the efforts of the captain to beach her. Eight hundred men were killed on board. When they arrived in Dunkirk, the Germans took many photos and filmed this elegant ship, with her still recognisable outline, stranded close to the beach covered with materiel and vehicles left behind by the Allies.

The shipwrecks of Operation Dynamo have not yet given up all of their secrets, far from it. Since September 2016, the Dunkirk diving club have undertaken archaeological research to find the wrecks of the *Doris* and *Lady Roseberry*, two British barges that sailed from Dover to take supplies to the men waiting to embark. At 3.30am on 1 June 1940, they sank off Malo-les-Bains after the tug towing them, the *St Fagan*, received a direct hit from a bomb which exploded in the engine room. Bruno Pruvost says that: *"The St Fagan sank almost immediately, taking with her the two barges she was towing. Only one barge survived, the Pudge, which picked up survivors."*

Entered into service in 1905, the *Devonia*, a 75-metre long paddle steamer, had seen service on the Bristol Channel before being requisitioned as minesweeper in 1914-1918. Before the Second World War, she made the Brighton–Boulogne-sur-Mer crossing. (Private collection.)

The wreck of the *Devonia*, seen here on 19 January 2015, lies to the east of the Zuydcoote beach, opposite the Bray-Dunes slipway. She is visible at each tide. (Private collection.)

The *Lorina*, a 89-metre long British passenger ship, entered into service in December 1918, made the pre-war Saint-Malo–Channel Islands crossing. She was requisitioned by the Royal Navy on 11 September 1939 as a troopship. She sailed for Dover at the start of Operation Dynamo. (Private collection.)

S. S. LORINA.   "COPYRIGHT SOUTHERN RAILWAY CO"

The wreck of the Lorina lies opposite the Malo-Terminus slipway. (Private collection.)

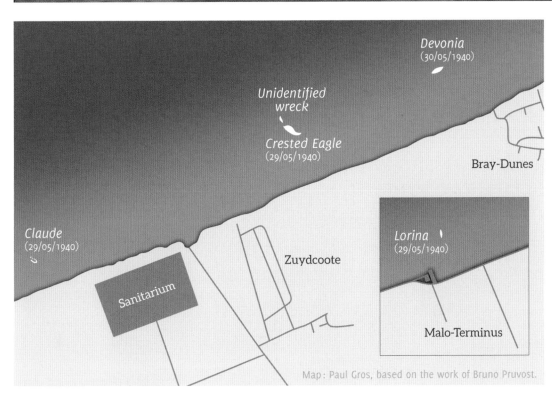

The emplacements of wrecks from Operation Dynamo visible at low tide at Dunkirk and the surrounding areas.

Devonia
(30/05/1940)

Unidentified wreck

Crested Eagle
(29/05/1940)

Bray-Dunes

Claude
(29/05/1940)

Zuydcoote

Sanitarium

Lorina
(29/05/1940)

Malo-Terminus

Map : Paul Gros, based on the work of Bruno Pruvost.

Annex The Fort des Dunes,
an actor and witness to the battle

Aerial view of the fort. One can see the extent to which the designers used the lay of the land. (Ville de Leffrinckoucke.)

The Fort des Dunes seen here after falling into German hands. One can see all of the vehicles left behind by the 12th motorised infantry division. (Laurent Decorte archives.)

Situated approximately one kilometre from the sea, in the municipality of Leffrinck-ouke, between Dunkirk and Zuydcoote, the Fort des Dunes still bears the traces of spring 1940 almost eighty years later. Bomb craters are still visible on the upper areas, even though grass has grown over them, and gaping wounds in the masonry shows that it was the target of German planes and artillery during Operation Dynamo.

It was a prime target. This defensive structure was built in 1878 as part of Séré de Rivières system. On 1 June, it was chosen by general Gaston Janssen to set up the staff headquarters of the 12th motorised infantry division. Having

fallen back from the Lille region, this division was tasked with defending the eastern part of the Dunkirk Pocket.

Late afternoon the following day, the fort came under attack from Stukas. Two bombs exploded in the officers courtyard. General Janssen received a mortal head wound; around him lay several dead or seriously wounded NCOs and officers. The commander of the 12th motorised infantry division was temporarily buried in a ditch, along with the other victims of the attack.

The suffering of the men in the fort was not over. During the morning of 3 June, a new *Luftwaffe* attack caused great damage and further victims. Following these attacks, which cost a hundred dead, the division's headquarters moved and set up in a school in the residential area near the Leffrinckouke train station.

The Germans took the fort on 4 June. After having cleared away the rubble and strengthened the masonry, the fort became part of the Atlantic Wall defences, along with the Zuydcoote battery that was built at the same time. The barracks housed the naval artillery personnel. However, the role of the fort did not stop there. On the parapet overlooking the service courtyard, the Germans installed a "*Würzburg See Reise Fumo 214*" type radar, the cupola of which measured 7.5 metres in diametre. This powerful radar was protected by flak set up around the fort. Also, the Organisation Todt built a bunker at the eastern-angle, below the escarpment wall.

On 6 September 1944, the fort was the scene of another dramatic event. Eight members of the local Resistance, arrested two days earlier, were shot in the north ditch, at the angle of the caponier. A plaque, placed by locality at the site of the executions, is a reminder of this tragic event.

German soldiers in front of one of the fort's buildings hit by bombs on 2 and 3 June. (Laurent Decorte archives.)

The ruins of the traverse shelter where, on 3 June, six of the 12th motorised infantry division's gendarmes were killed. (Erik Groult-Heimdal.)

After the surrender of the Dunkirk Pocket's garrison on 9 May 1945, the Fort des Dunes was used as an internment area for prisoners of war. It was then left abandoned for many years before being purchased by the locality of Leffrinckouke. Today, it houses a museum and is an example of late 19th century military architecture as well as a witness to the Second World War, from Operation Dynamo and through the years of occupation.

The buildings are remarkably well-integrated into the dune landscape. (Erik Groult-Heimdal.)

Annex When "Bebel" brought Operation Dynamo to the big screen

Based on Robert Merle's eponymous novel, winner of the 1949 Goncourt prize, the film, *Week-end à Zuydcoote*, was directed by Henri Verneuil in June and July 1964 and filmed where Operation Dynamo had taken place. The main roles were filled by Jean-Paul Belmondo, François Périer, Jean-Pierre Marielle and Pierre Mondy.

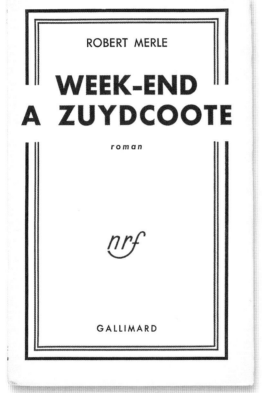

The novel, *Week-end à Zuydcoote*, won the Goncourt prize in 1949. (DR.)

ROBERT MERLE

WEEK-END A ZUYDCOOTE

roman

nrf

GALLIMARD

Robert Merle in 1964, the year the film was released. (DR.)

On Thursday 8 December 1949, a relatively unknown 49-year old, Robert Merle, won the most highly-coveted French book award, the Goncourt prize, for his first novel, *Week-end à Zuydcoote*, published by the prestigious Gallimard.

This first, but masterly novel, was not just a lucky first attempt. As well as its obvious literary quality, the book recalls a major event of the Second World War, but one that was mostly unknown to the wider public: Operation Dynamo. This was a subject that the author knew well. When war broke out, the author, born on 29 August 1908 at Tébessa (Algeria) worked as an English teacher and upon mobilisation, was attached to the British Expeditionary Force in a liaison role.

He experienced first hand the the tragic events of spring 1940. Arriving at Bray-Dunes on 27 May, the locality next to Zuydcoote, a locality ten kilometres north of Dunkirk, he received permission from a British general to embark that same day, but the boat ended up leaving without him. A good swimmer, he did not hesitate in trying several times to save from certain death wounded soldiers or those burned by flaming fuel. When the Germans entered Dunkirk on 4 June, he was taken prisoner in the cellars of the Zuydcoote sanitarium where he had taken shelter.

The novel was on the whole well-received by critics and the general public, but its publication nevertheless created a controversy of national consequences, but which was soon forgotten. Those who despised the book were led by the priest of Zuydcoote, *l'abbé* de Bonduaeux, a veteran of 14-18 who had witnessed first-hand the tragedy of May-June 1940, wrote in his parish magazine: *"The title of this book is an odious lie to which honest people end up believing. As for the author, he is a very bad egg. It is shameful that the name of our village, which was, in May 1940, a veritable field of heroism, be used to sell such despicable wild imaginings."* The man of the cloth continued: *"Concerning Mr Merle's book we shall not say much, this compilation of rudeness is only of interest to those who like trash."*

Although Robert Merle was new to his art, the same could not be said for Henri Verneuil. The film director, of Armenian origin (his real name was Achod Malakian), born on 15 October 1920 in Turkey, had already made several successful films when he decided to put *Week-end à Zuydcoote* on the big screen. Some of his films include: *La vache et le prisonier* (1959), *Le Président* (1961), *Un singe en hiver* (1962), *Mélodie en sous-sol* (1963) and *Cent mille dollars au soleil* (1964).

These vehicles used in the film were objects of curiosity for the local youth. (Private collection.)

It was not surprising that this craftsman of the silver screen and popular cinema, in its noblest sense, where action and psychology go hand in hand, was interested in Robert Merle's best-selling novel (re-published in paperback in 1966). With its highly dramatic historical backdrop and two-day timescale (Saturday 1 and Sunday 2 June) and its almost permanent set (the beach and the dunes), this novel, with all the suspense of a Greek tragedy, had all the ingredients needed to make good cinema.

Henri Verneuil chose someone he had known for a long time to play the main role, that of sergeant Julien Maillat, trapped in the Dunkirk Pocket where he would experience, over a short lapse of time, situations that were tragic, tender, heroic or comical. Jean-Paul Belmondo, the rising star of the time, was well-known to the director as he had recently been in *Un singe en hiver*, where he exchanged lines with Jean Gabin in unforgettable drunken scenes. He was also in *Cent mille dollars au soleil*, where "Bebel" (his nickname) played opposite Lino Ventura and Bernard Blier between drinks.

The actors cast as Belmondo's companions by Henri Verneuil were old hands of French cinema. Jean-Pierre Marielle was cast as l'abbé Pierson, the fatalistic and philosophical priest; François Périer was Alexandre, who played the homemaker to avoid thinking about his wife, who he missed painfully; and Pierre Mondy as Dhéry, resourceful and always able to find things to eat.

Also leading the cast were well-known faces such as Albert Rémy (Virrel, the corpse transporter), Georges Géret (Pinot, the light machine-gunner), Christian Barbier or Paul Préboist, playing other French soldiers. The beautiful Jeanne, who Julian Maillat saves from being raped, before she finally falls for him, is played by the gorgeous 21-year old Catherine Spaak, the niece of the Belgian deputy prime minister, Paul-Henri Spaak.

The film was a Franco-Italian production. Robert Merle, teaching at the Algiers university at the time, was brought in to help with the

adaptation, working on the script. When a journalist asked him if the film would be as spectacular as The Longest Day, which had come out two years earlier, Henri Verneuil was quick to say, *"No,* Week-end à Zuydcoote *will be totally different. This is not about a reconstitution. What I am interested in is the human side of the tragedy. This is what I am going to closely capture. In a way, it will be an anti-hero film. I will portray real characters, witnesses, capable of heroism, of course, but also cowardice. They are there on a strip of land but it was not their fault. It was an exceptional situation, but they will be seen as they really were."* [1]

The filming, using Eastmancolor 35mm colour film, began on Monday 1 June 1964 on a huge film set positioned at Bray-Dunes. Henri Verneuil stayed with his young wife in the "La Duine" villa, rented for the duration of the filming. All of the necessary equipment was also stored at Bray-Dunes, including seventy vehicles of all types purchased from Etablissements Cibié at Marquette-lez-Lille and mostly brought by road in a mixed convoy that caused quite a stir and which must have brought back memories, to some people, of the exodus of spring 1940.

As well as the cars and trucks, there were 155mm and 150mm guns, and a battery of 75mm artillery pieces, not forgetting three tanks, transported by rail and unloaded at the Bray-les-Dunes station. For the naval part, the team had two minesweepers, a merchant ship, a dozen trawlers, a pilot ship and twenty ships of various types. The aerial side was much more modest with three "Nord 102" aircraft disguised as Messerschmitt 109 fighters as they had a similar outline, flown by Alexandre Renault. The latter was stood in for by the famous stuntman Gilles Delamare in the spectacular scene where a German flyer parachutes from his plane and is killed with a burst of machine-gun fire by the brave Pinot, one of Belmondo-Maillat's companions.

In order to equip a thousand extras, no less than eleven tonnes of British uniforms (clothing, helmets, anklets, boots etc.) were bought from the famous Bermann establishment of London. There were also huge quantities of jackets, trousers, dresses, skirts, doctor's coats and nurse uniforms for the extras that would play the role of civilians. Dozens of dummies were also placed over the sands in order to portray the dead after a strafing or bombardment.

On the anniversary of the Normandy Landings on 6 June, the production team held a cocktail party for the film crew. This was the chance for Jean-Paul Belmondo, who was staying with a family in the "Clos Bleu" villa at Bray-Dunes, to inform the press that he had first been to Dunkirk twelve years earlier, when he was a pupil at the conservatory. Laid back as usual, "Bébel" kept on making schoolboy jokes with his actor friends with whom, it was said, he went on nocturnal excursions to nearby Belgium.

As well as the film set at Bray-Dunes, some streets in the same locality, the beach and dunes of Zuydcoote and Bray-Dunes, some scenes were filmed at the Rosendaël train station, which can be seen at the beginning of the film, and the sanitarium at Zuydcoote where thousands of wounded soldiers and civilians went to during the Battle of Dunkirk. Eighty years on, this huge cluster of red-bricked buildings, which is still in use, relived for the film the horror of the bombardments and fires, this time started by pyrotechnics and not by German artillery and planes. The head nurse, seen in the film counting the dead, accompanied by the doctor, Henri Verneuil, was played by a Red

Cross reservist nurse, Lucienne Pinte who ran, along with her husband, the estate agents tasked by the production team with accommodating the entire film crew.

As for the no less famous scene where Maillat and Pinot discover two German soldiers disguised as nuns in a ruined church, it was filmed

Top of the page: Filming on the beach. (Photo Depriester.)

Above: The beach today. (Photo Erik Groult-Heimdal.)

Extras gathered on the beach for filming. (Private collection.)

A tank used for the film, seen here arriving in the storage area for materiel, near the "Clos Fleuri" at Bray-Dunes. (Private collection.)

at Notre-Dame de Calais, bombed in the Second World War and restored in 2013.

The filming, at the places in Robert Merle's novel, ended on Thursday 30 July. The next day, Henri Verneuil caught the train for Paris at the Dunkirk station. Extra scenes were filmed over two weeks in a studio.

The film came out in French cinemas on Friday 18 December 1964. Over three million people saw the film and since, it has always received good viewing figures each time it is shown on television. This is what a journalist from the regional *La Voix du Nord* newspaper wrote: *"Henri Verneuil used huge resources, really huge resources. He has shown that with ships, planes, guns and thousands of extras that he*

Jean-Paul Belmondo seen here reading a newspaper, with his friend and body double, Maurice Auzel, a former French boxing champion. (Photo Neuts.)

A scene from the film. From left to right, Julien Maillat (Jean-Paul Belmondo), the priest (Jean-Pierre Marielle) and Alexandre (François Périer) at their improvised kitchen on the beach. (Private collection.)

knew how to make a blockbuster in the same way as Nicolas Ray or Darryl Zanuck. Even better than the latter, his blockbuster has retained a human element. In this we think of the scene that we think is the best of the entire film ; the sinking of a merchant ship full of soldiers who believed that they had at last escaped the hell of Dunkirk."[2]

Week-end à Zuydcoote was also successful abroad, shown in cinemas all over Europe, but also in America and Asia. In the United States and Great Britain, it was released under the title of Weekend at Dunkirk. The latter can be seen as a sort of nod to a certain Christopher Nolan

who, half a century later, would also pay tribute to the men trapped in the Dunkirk Pocket with his film Dunkirk...

---

(1) Week-end à Zuydcoote. 1964-2014, 50ᵉ anniversaire, Spécificités dunkerquoises, 2014. This well-researched and illustrated book helped us obtain most of the information used in this chapter.

(2) Ibid.

Above : A scene being filmed in the dunes. (Photo Depriester.)

Henri Verneuil, behind the camera directing the filming. (Private collection.)

The French film poster. The film came out in France on 18 December 1964 and was shown throughout the world. (Private collection.)

Above: Another French poster. (Private collection.)

A Belgian poster with an illustration that sums up Operation Dynamo. (Private collection.)

The English poster, with *Zuydcoote* replaced by *Dunkirk*. Like a nod to Christopher Nolan. (Private collection.)

DUNKIRK: JUNE, 1940...
366,000 ALLIED SOLDIERS...
TRAPPED WITH THE SEA ON
ONE SIDE...GERMAN ARMIES
ON THE OTHER—AND A
BEACHHEAD OF HELL IN BETWEEN!

*Not Since
"The Longest Day"
Has A Motion Picture
Recaptured Such
A Dramatic Moment
Of Courage
And Glory
In World War II!*

The poster made for the film' fiftieth anniversary in 2014. (Private collection.)

Zuydcoote, a name made famous in France and abroad thanks to literature and cinema. Seen here is the front of the train station, now un-used, and which is now a pharmacy. (Photo Erik Groult-Heimdal.)

Annex Christopher Nolan brings back the Dunkirk Spirit

Dunkirk returned to the past in spring 2016. Christopher Nolan, the famous director of *Insomnia, the Dark Knight* trilogy and *Interstellar*, arrived to film Dunkirk, a big-budget American, British and French production based on Operation Dynamo.

23 May 2016. The first day of filming on the beach at Leffrinckoucke. Each extra is holding a cardboard cutout simulating several soldiers. (Private collection.)

The afternoon of 23 May. The public watches the filming in the rue Belle-Rade. (Photo Ville de Dunkerque.)

In order to bring these events back to life, Nolan looks at the intertwined fates of three British soldiers who eventually succeed, after various setbacks, in getting back to England.

In an interview, Christopher Nolan stated that: *"Dunkirk is one of the biggest stories in human history to be portrayed in cinema.(...) I wanted to use my IMAX camera in order to plunge the spectator into this incredible odyssey. The film puts the viewer into the shoes of someone who was on the beach, in the cockpit of a Spitfire pilot, on the deck of a civilian yacht entering into hell.(...) It is an odyssey in IMAX, virtual reality without the special glasses."*

In late 2015, Christopher Nolan went to Dunkirk to study the area. This trip convinced him to film where the events had taken place. According to the deputy mayor of Dunkirk, Michel Tomasek, in charge of culture and heritage, *"Nolan was won over by Dunkirk, despite the fact that with modern technology he could have filmed somewhere else, notably on the English coast. The fact that he chose Dunkirk went down very well, not only with local politicians, but also with the population."*

An air attack has just disrupted embarkation. For this scene, the bomb explosions were created by setting off explosives placed under the sand and detonated from a distance. (Photo Ville de Dunkerque.)

As well as the places, Nolan also wanted the inhabitants to take part in his new adventure. Some 1,500 extras were taken on out of 4,500 applications sent to the town hall in February 2016. Some of the criteria set were as follows: to be no taller than 1m83cm and to look like someone from the period. Amongst the lucky candidates were 50-year old Bruno Pruvost and his two sons, Emmanuel, 30 and Quentin, 23. The third son did not apply as he is 1m87cm tall.

"The key to being taken on was to say that you were very available", explained Bruno Pruvost, who spent a day filming on the beach, dressed as a British soldier and like his comrades, held a cardboard cutout of the outline of several Tommies to multiply the number of men on the screen. Despite having to arrive at the Dunkirk exhibition hall at 5.30am and setting up on the beach at 6.30am, Bruno, who has been fascinated by Operation Dynamo and its shipwrecks since he arrived in Dunkirk at the age of seven, has great memories of this experience. *"Knowing Week-end à Zuydcoote, a film I love, by heart, it was a no-brainer to apply. I was impressed by the excellent organisation. What really moved me was going back in time thirty years to when I did my military service, with people from all backgrounds and all ages, all dressed the same and waving to the planes that*

Christopher Nolan, centre, directing the extras on the beach. (Photo Ville de Dunkerque.)

A British soldier shooting at a German plane. (Photo Ville de Dunkerque.)

A British soldier shooting at a German plane. (Photo Ville de Dunkerque.)

The "Little Ships" arrive at the beach. (Photo Ville de Dunkerque.)

flew over, or all of us throwing ourselves onto the sand. It was an honour for me to take part in this film."

Emmanuel also worked as an extra for a day but his brother, Quentin, had four. One of these was notably Monday 30 May when rain, wind and cold battered the extras lined up on the East Mole, reconstituted as it looked in 1940 by the film's construction crew. Another extra, present that day, posted the following on social media:

"It was horrible. We had the wind and rain gusting in our faces. Nolan made us all walk along the mole in an apocalyptic and unbearable atmosphere. Some extras even had to leave as they could not bear it any longer. Nolan and his crew were at the end of the mole and we were all herded there in front of him. It was then that I realised why he did not want us to go and warm up throughout the day. He wanted us to suffer, for us to look like real soldiers, and

Above: A Spitfire flying close to the beach. The film crew also had radio-controlled smaller size aircraft for the aerial scenes. (Photo Ville de Dunkerque.)

Below: An explosion at the East Mole. The film's construction crew built a wooden jetty, painted white, as it would have looked in 1940. (Photo Ville de Dunkerque.)

British soldiers ready to embark from the mole. (Photo Ville de Dunkerque.)

A Citroën U23 truck used in the film. (photo Damien Bouet-Collection Normandie Rétro Prestige.)

blimey, I can guarantee you that was the case." It goes without saying that the buses brought in by the director for the troops to shelter and warm up in after this moment of derring-do, were most welcome.

The filming at Dunkirk was spread over twenty-four days, under the code-name of "*Bodrega Bay*" in reference to Alfred Hitchcock's film, *The Birds*; a director held in high esteem by Nolan. The clapper board first sounded on the morning of 23 May 2016 on the beach at Leffrinckouke. Filming continued that afternoon at Malo-les-Bains in rue Belle-Rade and rue des Fusillés. The other days were mostly spent filming scenes on the beaches, at sea, or in the port.

Making an historical film is always a more of less difficult technical challenge. For the aerial

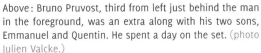

Above: Bruno Pruvost, third from left just behind the man in the foreground, was an extra along with his two sons, Emmanuel and Quentin. He spent a day on the set. (photo Julien Valcke.)

scenes, Nolan used full-size aircraft, notably several period Spitfires, but also radio-controlled smaller planes. On screen, the high-pitched sound of these mini Stukas and Messerschmitts was of course replaced by a more realistic sound.

Several military ships were also used, such as the *Maillé-Brézé*, a former French destroyer and a floating museum since 1988, and several Dutch navy ships, also dating from the 1950s. Amongst the latter was the *Sittard*, a Dutch navy cadet school ship, which played the role of two British ships. With the pennant number H 32 on the port side, it was *HMS Havant*, sunk during Operation Dynamo. On the starboard side, it bore the pennant number F 34 for HMS Jaguar, which evacuated some seven hundred soldiers on 28 May 1940.

Many British boats were also brought over, notably for the scenes where we see the "Little Ships" arriving from England. Some of these small craft had really taken part in Operation Dynamo, such as the torpedo boat MTB 102, built in 1937 and which had the honour of taking on board Churchill and Eisenhower when they inspected the allied fleet in 1944 before it set sail for Normandy.

The film construction crew also went as far as to build the wreck of the *Adroit*, the French destroyer beached at Malo-les-Bains during the night of 20-21 May and cut in two when her cargo of shells blew up.

As well as the extras, the people of Dunkirk were also interested in the spectacular filming, waiting patiently and using their guile in order to follow the various scenes and catch a glimpse of the actors. Of particular interest was Harry Styles, one of the film's main characters and famous for being part of the pop group One Direction.

The final takes at Dunkirk were filmed on 23 June. Afterwards, the film crew left for Holland, then southern England to film extra naval and aerial scenes.

Emmanuel Pruvost, 30, on the far right of the photo. He spent a day as an extra on the set. (photo Julien Valcke.)

Acknowledgements

This book owes much to the warm and cooperative welcome of our Dunkirk contacts from the beginning to the end of this fascinating editorial adventure. We would like to extend our thanks to the town of Dunkirk, notably to Jean-Yves Frémont, deputy mayor in charge of integration, economic development and tourism for port affairs; to Michel Tomasek, deputy mayor in charge of culture and heritage; Patrick Vaesken, head of territorial strategy and development; to Sabine L'Hermet, head of the tourism office, Laurence Baillieul, press relations officer; the town's archives and research department; Lucien Dayan, president of the Mémorial du Souvenir association; Eric Debril, head of service for culture, heritage, tourism, fetes and ceremonies for the town of Leffrinckouke; the municipality of Zuydcoote; Bruno Pruvost, specialist in Operation Dynamo shipwrecks; Laurent Decorte, collector of period objects and photos; the municipality of Esquelbecq; Thibaut Grimaldi, collector of period vehicles; Gérard Cerizier and Stéphane Chesneaux for their contribution to the pages concerning uniforms; Damien Bouet for his photos of period vehicles; Erik Groult, our companion during our trip to Dunkirk and, finally, Paul Gros (graphic artist and layout), Thierry Vallet (for the plane profiles), and all the team at Heimdal publishers.

Sources

ECPAD archives for the British Expeditionary Force in France

Robert Béthegnies, *Le sacrifice de Dunkerque 1940*, Yves Demailly éditeur, Lille, 1947

Robert Béthegnies, *La défense de Dunkerque 1940*, Yves Demailly éditeur, Lille, 1950

David Divine, *Les 9 jours de Dunkerque*, Calmann-Lévy, 1964

François de Lannoy, *Dunkerque 1940*, Heimdal, 2004

Eric Lefèvre, *Dunkerque, la bataille des dunes*, Charles Lavauzelle, 1981

Jean-Marc Alcalay, *La plume et le fusil*, Ysec éditions, 2008

Olivier Vermesch, *Les fusillés du fort des Dunes*, éditions La Voix du Nord, 1994

Serge Blanckaert, *L'infernale bataille de Dunkerque, mai-juin 1940*, éditions Le Phare, 1977

Alan Brooke, *L'espoir change de camp*, Plon, 1959

Général Armengaud, *Le drame de Dunkerque, mai-juin 1940*, Plon, 1948

Week-end à Zuydcoote, 1964-2014, Spécificités dunkerquoises, 2014

Histoire du fort des Dunes, Ville de Leffrinckoucke, 1999

Places of interest

Musée Dunkerque 1940 – Opération Dynamo: on the site of the former Bastion 32, HQ of French forces.

Dynamo Tour: A visit by minibus around the main sites of Operation Dynamo, put on by the Dunkirk tourism office.

Dkepaves.free.fr: A fascinating and educational internet site on the shipwrecks of Operation Dynamo.

Fort des Dunes (Leffrinckoucke): One of the main sites of Operation Dynamo and the German occupation, now a museum.

Printed in February 2018 by Pulsio at Sofia (Bulgaria)
for Éditions Heimdal, Georges Bernage, publisher.